FINAL BREAKTHROUGH!

Arthur toweled himself dry of the sweat produced by the 90-degree weather and three long sets of losing tennis. He quickly changed shirts and then waited impatiently for Bob Lutz to reappear.

"Don't you want to wash up and rest?" the referee asked.

"Nope. I just want to get going."

It was a highly unusual move, but Arthur was anxious to get back to the match. He did not want to relax mentally. He was determined not to let the top ranking slip away from him now. Not after all this time.

Bob Lutz came back from the locker room, ready to continue. After only a few shots in the fourth set, it became obvious to those watching that something about the match was different. Suddenly, it was all Ashe. Ace after ace tore off Arthur's racket. Winning volley after winning volley crashed past Lutz. Two sets later, the crown was Arthur's 4–6, 6–3, 8–10, 6–0, 6–4. That afternoon at the Longwood Cricket Club Richmond's most famous athlete had become the world's amateur tennis champion.

ARTHUR ASHE: TENNIS CHAMPION
was originally published by
Doubleday & Company, Inc.

Critics' Corner:

"A good sports biography...."

—Bulletin of the Center for Children's Bc
University of Chicago

"Highly recommended."

—We Build Together, third revision, edited b
Charlemae Rollins (NCTE publication)

"Arthur Ashe is a tennis natural ... the first male Negro to make the big time in a stronghold of white "gentlemen".... Mr. Robinson details the development of a tennis star with appropriate attention to the discipline and hard work demanded.... From the time Arthur, at six, first caught the attention of the Richmond park instructor, he had something—and a succession of tennis enthusiasts recognized and nurtured his talent.... Arthur Ashe is currently seeded No. 1, and kids who couldn't care less about tennis will be following his career. How and why it happened are all here."

—The Kirkus Reviews

Also recommended by: Bro-Dart Foundation, Elementary School Library Collection.

About the Author:

LOUIE ROBINSON, JR. is the West Coast bureau chief of *Ebony* magazine. Born in Dallas, Texas, he attended public schools there. He studied for two years at Lincoln University, in Jefferson City, Missouri before he entered the army in World War II. His principal work, since leaving the army, has been writing and working for magazines. He has written both fiction and nonfiction for such publications as *Ebony, Jet, Negro Digest* and *Tan.* Mr. Robinson's hobby is photography. He also likes to travel, and his work has taken him throughout the United States and to Mexico.

ARTHUR ASHE
Tennis Champion

——— • ———

by Louie Robinson, Jr.

AN ARCHWAY PAPERBACK
POCKET BOOKS • NEW YORK

ARTHUR ASHE: Tennis Champion

Doubleday edition published 1967

Archway Paperback edition published July, 1969

5th printing .... August, 1975

L

Published by
POCKET BOOKS, a division of Simon & Schuster, Inc.,
630 Fifth Avenue, New York, N.Y.

Archway Paperback editions are distributed in the
U.S. by Simon & Schuster, Inc., 630 Fifth Avenue,
New York, N.Y. 10020, and in Canada by Simon &
Schuster of Canada, Ltd., Markham, Ontario, Canada.

Standard Book Number: 671-29754-6.

CONTENTS

Photographs appear between pages 64 and 65.

PICTURE CREDITS

Courtesy of the Ashe family: pictures 1-4, 6.

Australian News and Information Bureau: pictures 28, 29 (Henk Brusse).

Ebony Magazine: pictures 7 (Maurice Sorrell), 8, 10.

Photos by Ed Fernberger: pictures 5, 11, 13, 14, 16, 18, 27.

Picture 26: John Zimmerman LIFE Magazine © Time Inc.

United Press International: pictures 20, 21, 22, 23, 24, 25.

Wide World Photos: pictures 15, 17, 19.

World Tennis Magazine: 9, 12 (P. W. Trostorff).

Excerpt from "If" by Rudyard Kipling. Copyright 1910 by Rudyard Kipling. From *Rudyard Kipling's Verse: Definitive Edition*. Reprinted by permission of Doubleday & Company, Inc. and Mrs. George Bambridge.

The editors wish to specially acknowledge *World Tennis* Magazine for all of the aid which their staff so generously provided.

Chapter 1

NOTHING RIGHT

"Didn't I tell you never to sass anyone?"

Arthur Ashe's father, his face drawn into a frown, stood looking down at his young son.

"I didn't, I didn't."

"Then why do they come to me and complain about you?" his father asked.

"I was there first. They tried to chase me off, but I wouldn't go."

"How long had you been there?"

"That's not a fair question," Arthur said. "You know the rule. If you get to the practice board first, you can stay as long as you want."

"Son, there is just that one practice board for all of Brookfield Park. Rule or no rule, one skinny little boy like you isn't supposed to hog it all day. Next time, don't cause trouble, hear? If you do, you won't be allowed in the park at all."

Six-year-old Arthur Ashe looked up at his father

1

and nodded his head. Yes, he would try not to get into any more trouble. He couldn't give up the park, give up the practice board, give up tennis now that he had found an answer to the lonely days.

Only months ago, Arthur's home had been filled with happiness. Small and simply furnished, it was warm with family love. There had been Arthur, his younger brother Johnny, his father Arthur Senior, and his mother Mattie.

Like other Negroes in Richmond, Virginia, the Ashe family lived in the "colored" section of town. Arthur went to a different school than the white children and played in a different playground.

But Arthur's father had been luckier than most Negro men, who found it hard to get anything but second class jobs. Mr. Ashe had been made a special police officer in charge of Brookfield Park, and his family lived in a house inside the park itself.

Here Arthur and his buddies could pretend they were kings. They had shade trees, horse shoe pits, and baseball diamonds. They even had a basketball court, a football field, a swimming pool, and tennis courts.

The fact that their darker skins set them apart did not bother Arthur and his friends. They were too busy playing after school and getting home in time for supper to worry about any world outside their own—if they even suspected there was another world.

As far back as Arthur could remember, he had never heard his mother and father speak crossly to one another or quarrel, and they rarely got really angry at Arthur or his brother Johnny, although both boys caused their share of mischief. Each boy seemed to know that if he was told to do something and it was important, he should obey. The worst punishment for Arthur was feeling that his parents were disappointed in him.

He didn't even like to remember the day he had disobeyed his mother on purpose and had gone roaming off to the other end of Brookfield Park with a friend. It was a late afternoon in the fall and by the time the two young travelers had reached the far side of the park, it was already dark.

"I'm going home," Arthur said, realizing that his mother would not only be furious with him for having gone so far, but that she would be worried, too.

"You crazy? It's spooky in that park at night," his friend said.

"I don't care, I'm going."

Alone and frightened, Arthur made his way back. He had never been so far from home without having someone with him. In the darkness, the shadows of the trees and bushes seemed to be waiting to snatch him. At first he walked fast, but finally his fear got the better of him and he began to run.

By the time he reached home, everyone in the neighborhood was out looking for him. His mother was in tears. Seeing her cry made him ache. He hadn't meant to disobey her and go off that way. He tried to explain this to his father.

"Your mother and I and all these people have been looking for you for hours, boy."

Half crying, Arthur tried to tell his parents that he was sorry. He hadn't meant to hurt anybody. As he spoke, he kept thinking how nice his mother always was to him. He couldn't imagine why he had worried her.

He lay awake that night thinking about everything that had happened. He almost wished his father had hit him or said something really stern to him. But Mr. Ashe hadn't. He had simply sent Arthur straight off to bed. "As though they didn't want even to look at me," Arthur thought.

That was a bad time. Arthur promised himself that such a thing would never happen again. He told his father and mother of his promise, and things went along smoothly again until one day when Arthur's mother stayed home from her job at the department store. She was "just resting a little," she told her son when he asked her why she hadn't gone to work.

"You aren't sick, are you, Mother?"

4

"I'm just a bit tired," she said, gently brushing the top of his head with her hand. "You run along now. Haven't you got a baseball game?"

Arthur dug his baseball bat and glove out of the closet, pulled on a sweater, and was out the door in no time.

Later, Arthur learned from his father that his mother was ill and that she had to have an operation. But even then, no one could have expected what was to happen. On the way back to her room in the hospital after the operation, Mrs. Ashe suffered a stroke. For six days she lay quiet in her bed. No medicine seemed to do any good. The next morning, with the doctor and Mr. Ashe standing beside her, unable to help, she died.

Everything in Arthur's life seemed changed. One moment it had all been fine. Then, suddenly, nothing was right anymore. It was as though nothing would ever be right again.

That was when the lonely days began.

Chapter 2

LIFE WITHOUT A MOTHER

Arthur didn't go to his mother's funeral. "I don't want to see Mama that way," he told his father. The only funeral Arthur had ever been to was his grandfather's. Even now the memory of the old man lying there so still sent chills through him.

"You don't have to go if you don't want to," Mr. Ashe comforted him. "Just be a good boy."

The March winds were cutting and bitter, and everyone who came to visit brought the cold in with him, exposing every corner of the living room to it. Arthur watched the people closely as they came and went, some weeping, some sad and quiet. He knew his father wouldn't have much time to talk to him now, and it made Arthur feel small and alone. Sometimes he would stand near the window, where he could look out and see a tall, slender young man hitting a ball against the practice board on the tennis courts. One day, that same young man, Ronald Charity, would be Arthur's closest companion, but now he was just someone to watch, someone to help Arthur forget.

The young man stroked the ball toward the board with his racket in a regular pattern. Then, as the ball bounced back, he would get himself into position so that he could stroke it toward the board once more. The young man was alone, too, Arthur thought to himself, but he didn't seem to mind it. He was completely wrapped up in what he was doing.

As Arthur watched from the window, he thought he would like to try the man's game. Perhaps it would help make things all right again.

As it turned out, it would be some time before things were all right again in the Ashe household. Trying to be both mother and father to two young sons and to keep his home in order and get to work on time was more than Mr. Ashe could handle. Neither of the boys was big enough to help, and Johnny was too young even to understand that his mother had died.

"Isn't Mother ever coming back, Daddy?" Johnny asked his father one night.

Arthur saw his father make believe he hadn't heard Johnny and walk into another room. Arthur wondered if his father was going to be sick, too.

It was only a few nights later that Mr. Ashe tried to explain to Arthur and Johnny that their daddy needed a rest. He told them that they were going to live with relatives for a while.

"I don't want to go. I want to stay with you," Johnny pleaded.

"We will all be back together soon," their father promised.

"We don't want to go," the two children insisted.

"I know you don't. I don't want you to go, either. But right now, you have to. You won't have to stay there long. Now, off to bed."

Arthur watched from the bedroom door as Mr. Ashe packed his sons' clothes in a big suitcase. If Arthur bit down hard on his lips, he found he could force back tears. But when the time came to leave, even biting his lips didn't help. He was too upset. He couldn't even look back or wave to his father, standing alone in the bus station.

Life away from home was lonely and sad for both Arthur and his brother. Every time their father came to visit them, they pleaded with him to take them back. Arthur would have given almost anything to go home. He could hardly believe his father wasn't teasing him when one day he said that the three of them would soon be together again.

The ride back to Richmond was a joy. Arthur

had never felt happier. But then Mr. Ashe told the two boys about the old lady he had found to take care of them.

"I don't want a servant," their father said. "I invited Mrs. Berry—that's the lady's name, Mrs. Otis Berry—to come live with us because I wanted someone who would be just like one of the family."

Arthur didn't like the idea at all. He thought he and his father and Johnny could make out fine together.

"I promised her one thing, though, and I know you boys are going to help me prove I mean what I say," Mr. Ashe continued. "I promised her that if she did stay, she would be the boss of the house."

Arthur could see that Johnny wasn't the least bit bothered by anything his father had said. He supposed that Johnny was just too young to understand. How could his father talk this way? How could he bring anyone in to take his mother's place? Wasn't he supposed to be the boss of their house?

Arthur didn't even say "hello" when his father introduced Mrs. Berry, and he stood silent when Mr. Ashe told his sons in front of "that lady" that he wanted them to call her "Mother."

"Mother?" The word stuck in Arthur's throat. He would never call her "Mother." Mrs. Berry was

10

a complete stranger. Perhaps Johnny could say the word easily, but Arthur could remember his own mother.

"I won't do it," he told himself.

Mr. Ashe, happy at having his sons home again, was preparing for a party. "Get out the ice cream and cake," he said. "Let's celebrate."

"I'm not hungry," Arthur said stiffly. "I want to go to bed."

"Don't you feel well, son?"

"I'm just tired," Arthur answered, upset by the attention he was getting.

"You mean to tell me that you are too tired to eat ice cream?" Mr. Ashe asked.

"I'm just tired," Arthur repeated.

"All right, boy. It *has* been a long day for you."

Arthur knew his father was disappointed. He hated to hurt him, but he couldn't stand this old lady and he wouldn't call her "Mother." Quietly, he went off to bed.

Mrs. Berry, Arthur soon learned, was a gentle woman of both wit and courage. She was always ready to accept new challenges—even the ones that he and his brother offered her.

Often, Mrs. Berry would tell the Ashe boys to do something, or not to do something, so that they would always be able to "walk with their heads high and backs straight," just as she did. She said she could look any man or woman in the eye without feeling guilty, for she had never spread or listened to mean talk about anyone. Arthur knew this was probably true because of the way she went after Johnny and him whenever they told on each other. She would "have no part of such tattling," she said.

Still, Arthur had promised himself never to like her. The first weeks were uncomfortable for everyone. No matter what Mrs. Berry tried to help him with, the six-year-old Arthur snapped at her.

"I'm a big boy, I can do it myself," he would say, and he fussed and complained when his father continued to demand he call the strange old woman "Mother."

"She's not my mother, not my real mother," he told himself. "She can't tell me what to do."

But Mr. Ashe was as good as his word. He was that kind of man, and he would never ask his sons to do what he was not prepared to do himself. If he demanded that Mrs. Berry's opinions and decisions be treated with respect by his children, he would do the same. "There's no sense making laws or bargains if you don't intend to keep them," he would say. Mr. Ashe always kept his bargains.

One Saturday, Arthur's father gave up a hunting trip he had been planning for days because Mrs. Berry didn't think he should go. They had all awakened early that morning, and Mr. Ashe had jumped out of bed and dressed quickly, pulling on his warmest clothing and boots to protect himself against the winter cold. The snow was already beginning to fall as Arthur watched his father take his rifle from the closet and begin to button his winter jacket. Thin white flakes dotted the icy window sills and frosted the tops of the trees outside the house. Mr. Ashe was almost at the door when Mrs. Berry called to him.

"Mr. Ashe, I don't think you should go hunting today. It looks as though the weather might get very bad before long."

"Okay, Mother," was all his father had said to her, as he turned around, put his gun away, and took off his heavy jacket. Arthur wondered if his father felt some of the anger that Arthur himself so often felt when Mrs. Berry interfered with his plans.

But Mrs. Berry hadn't lived seventy-two years without learning something about six-year-olds and their feelings. When Mr. Ashe would ask if the boys were minding her, she would say that he was out of order to ask such a thing.

"You've got good boys," she would say. "You have no call even to suspect them of being anything less."

To her, Arthur was a quiet little boy who was still grieving for his mother. She knew he would

13

come around if she were patient and allowed him to decide to do so by himself. He just needed time.

If she asked him what he would like for supper and he answered, "I don't care. I don't like the way you cook anyhow," she would tell him in a joking way that she was certain the Good Lord would reward him one day for putting up with her poor efforts.

If he wouldn't wear a shirt or a pair of shorts because she "didn't know how to sew them right," she would laugh and say it was true, and ask him to try to bear with her until she learned how.

If he refused to let her help him put a bandage on a cut, or tie a shoe lace, or button his coat, she would tell him she was glad he was big enough to take care of himself.

Little by little, Arthur came to realize that Mrs. Berry was doing the best she could to take the place of the mother he had lost. Mrs. Berry told him what to do, Arthur decided, because someone had to. For as long as was necessary, he would try to make the best of it.

Meanwhile, he could find escape in the big park, at the horse shoe pits, down by the swimming pool, in a game of baseball, and maybe even on the concrete tennis courts where the tall young man came to practice every day.

Chapter 3

ARTHUR MAKES A FRIEND

Ronald Charity stopped working on the practice board long enough to wipe the sweat out of his eyes and sneak a closer look at the small boy who had been watching him for so long. He had seen the child before—many times—running around the playground, usually playing baseball.

More than once Ronald had stopped by the baseball diamond to watch in amusement as the boy swung at the air with a bat almost as big as himself. Many times, too, he had seen the boy studying him as he practiced his tennis.

Arthur Ashe, Junior, looked small for his age. "Sixty pounds of bare bone," Ronald said to himself with a smile. Today Arthur was carrying a tennis racket.

"That racket is about as big as you are, young fellow," Ronald called to Arthur as he walked over to him.

"It's my daddy's," Arthur replied.

15

"What's your name?" Ronald asked.

"Arthur Ashe, Junior," the boy spoke out with pride. "What's yours?"

"Mr. Charity, Ronald Charity."

Ronald Charity had been employed by the Richmond Recreation Department to teach tennis at Brookfield Park during the summer. He was working his way through Virginia Union University and had taken the job because he loved to play tennis and because he needed all the money he could earn for the coming year.

"It would be impossible to teach tennis to anyone that young," Ronald thought to himself as he talked to the boy. But then, Ronald Charity had been doing the impossible for years. Ronald hadn't been very much older than Arthur when he had taught himself to play tennis with the help of nothing more than a "how-to" book. He had read in the newspaper that one of his school mates had won a local tennis tournament—a contest in which many players are matched against each other—and he had decided then and there that "if that kid can win a tennis tournament, so can I." He saved up, bought the book, borrowed a racket, and began. It took him some time to learn the game, but he taught himself well enough to win some of those tournaments he had read about in the newspaper. So, if a little voice inside Ronald Charity said "impossible," Ronald knew better.

"Do you want me to show you how to hit the ball?" he asked.

"Yes, sir!" Arthur answered.

"Okay, come on out on the court and give it a try. The first thing you have to learn is how to hold the racket properly."

"Yes, sir!" Arthur said again, eagerly, and he followed his new friend onto the court.

"There's a trick to making sure your hand is in the proper place on the racket," Ronald explained. "You just stand your racket on its rim, like so, and then take the handle in your hand, like this, and you can't go wrong."

Arthur watched his teacher closely, trying to do exactly what Ronald told him.

"Now," Ronald was saying, "push your hand as far down on the handle as you can without changing the position of your hand or making your grip uncomfortable. It's best if you can get your palm behind it." Ronald held out his hand so that Arthur could see exactly how the end of the racket should rest in his palm.

"Okay," Ronald went on, "now that you've got the grip right, try swinging the racket straight back, then straight forward, about hip high."

Arthur swung the racket back and forth just as Mr. Charity had told him.

"Good." Ronald put a hand on Arthur's shoulder. "When you hit the ball that way, it's called a *forehand drive.*

"Now," Ronald continued, "you see how to hit a forehand shot. That stroke is okay if the ball bounces in front of you or to your right, but what are you going to do if the ball bounces on your left side?"

Arthur looked at him and shook his head.

"Simple. You just turn your body around like this." Ronald turned on his left foot so that his right hip, rather than his left, now faced the net. "You switch your grip on the racket so that your thumb is behind the handle. This stroke is called a *backhand drive.* Okay, you try it."

Arthur copied Ronald's motion perfectly. It surprised the young man to see such a small boy do so well.

"Can we play now?" Arthur asked. He was in a hurry to begin hitting the ball the way Ronald Charity did.

"Soon," Ronald promised.

And so they went on, the young man explaining the proper way to hit the ball, the little boy watching closely and following the instructions carefully.

The first time Arthur had ever tried to hit a tennis ball, he had taken the racket in both hands like a baseball bat and had swung at the ball with all his might. He had thrown himself at the ball so wildly that, although he had managed to hit it, he had fallen down on the court. Now, with Ronald Charity guiding him, Arthur quickly learned that you didn't hit a tennis ball like a baseball, you *stroked* it.

"Hey," Ronald yelled to Arthur, as the boy once again took a full swing at the ball and sent it flying over the fence, "there aren't any home runs in tennis, you know."

Arthur listened while his teacher explained that "you have to learn how to stroke the ball properly in a kind of slow motion before you can hope to hit it hard."

His next try was much better, and the one after that was even better. Each time Arthur hit the ball, Ronald would tell him what he had done wrong, and the next time Arthur would dig in and try harder. In the beginning, Arthur often hit the ball out of the court, sending his teacher into fits of laughter.

"How can a little boy like you hit that ball so far and so hard?" Ronald would ask.

But slowly Arthur learned how to keep his shots in the court, and soon he was driving the ball very well.

"That kid's size and age don't seem to matter at all," he heard Ronald tell another man.

Arthur liked learning how to play tennis, but most of all he liked Ronald Charity. And so every afternoon he made his way to the tennis courts to practice hitting the ball against the practice board by himself.

Arthur soon became the most familiar figure at the Brookfield Park tennis courts, but he was far from the most popular one.

"Ronald Charity may find him amusing, but we don't," the older people would say. "He always keeps us waiting for a court."

"Pest" was the favorite word for Arthur among the teen-age set, particularly when Arthur would answer their demands to give up his court with "First come, first served." The only way to get Arthur away from the courts and the practice board, they decided, was to chase him.

One afternoon Arthur got to the tennis courts early. No one had come back from lunch yet, but Arthur knew it wouldn't be long before the whole park would be alive with noise, and people would be waiting to use the courts. He wished Ronald were there, so that they could play before anyone else came.

Arthur began hitting the ball against the practice board. Whenever he hit it too high and sent it flying over the fence, he had to run outside and around the courts to get it back.

Once while he was off looking for his ball, an

older boy and girl arrived at the courts and began to use the practice board.

"Hey, I'm using that," Arthur yelled to them as he ran back to the practice area.

"Yeah? Well, we are using it now," the big boy answered.

"That's not fair. You two can play on the court. I have to practice here until Mr. Charity comes."

"Beat it!" the older boy growled.

Arthur wanted to fight for his rights, but how could a seven-year-old fight such a big boy? He decided, instead, to pay no attention to the boy and girl. He would just go right on with what he had been doing.

Acting as though there was no one else around, Arthur approached the narrow board and began practicing. Soon both balls were bounding back toward the bigger boy at once, making it impossible for him to hit either one.

"Get out of here!" the boy yelled at Arthur, taking a swing at the youngster with his racket.

But Arthur, experienced in such matters, had already jumped back out of reach, and he began to laugh at the older boy's fury. That was just enough to drive the older boy and girl to more serious action.

"Why don't you take his racket away from him?" the girl suggested. "He's nothing but a pest."

21

The chase was on. Almost before the girl had spoken, Arthur guessed what was coming. He picked up his tennis ball and began to run. Around the tennis court the three went, seven-year-old Arthur in the lead, but only a step or two ahead. Finally Arthur ran around the net and over to the door. Before the other two could grab him, he was free and away.

He darted off between the two great maple trees near the fence, to the vast lawns beyond. The boy and girl stayed close behind for a while, but soon gave up. Arthur ran on until, with a final burst of speed, he fell exhausted on the cool grass, his body and clothes wet with sweat. He lay there for a few minutes, looking up at the sky and thinking about what he might be when he grew up, and about Mr. Charity, and finally about his mother.

Then he rolled over and closed his eyes. He thought about the garbage men, whom he often watched in the morning while they picked up the heavy trash cans and tossed them into the truck. Some day, when he grew up, he'd be a garbage man. Garbage men were big and strong. No one would ever bother him them.

"What on earth are you doing, boy?" It was the sharp voice of his father.

"Just thinking," Arthur answered.

"Thinking about what?" his father asked.

"Nothing," came the answer.

"Get up here, boy," Mr. Ashe said. "Come on. I want to talk to you."

Arthur couldn't remember anything that he had done wrong recently. Still, he knew his father wanted to talk about something important. He could tell from the way his father looked and spoke, and even from the way he walked toward the benches near the baseball diamond. He walked ahead of Arthur instead of with him.

"Arthur," his father said sternly, "how many times have I told you not to bother the older people over at the tennis courts and not to talk back to anybody? I told you to come to me if you had any trouble over there."

"I didn't talk back to anyone," Arthur protested. "I was there first. They came after I did and chased me away from the practice board."

"There's a boy and girl over there who say you yelled some bad things at them, and that you bothered them while they were trying to play," Arthur's father replied.

Arthur shook his head. "It's not true," he told his father. And then he explained all that had happened.

"Arthur," the boy's father said softly but seriously, "if I have told you once, I have told you a hundred times, I don't want you giving anyone sass. If someone tells you to leave the courts, you just come to me and let me handle it."

"But I don't sass anyone, Daddy," Arthur answered.

"Well, just you see that you don't." His father got up to leave. "I want you to grow up to be a fine young man and a gentleman first. *Then* you can be a tennis player or anything else you want to be."

Arthur nodded and watched his father walk off toward the pool. He didn't follow. He decided to stay where he was for a while before going back to the courts to look for Ronald Charity.

Ronald had come along just when he had most needed a friend, someone who could be like an older brother to him. As Arthur waited, he tried to think what it would be like if his father told him he couldn't spend his afternoons with Ronald at the courts. He remembered the lonely times and he thought about his mother. She had been on his mind all day.

"Hey?" Ronald Charity's voice brought a sudden end to Arthur's thoughts. "Where have you been?"

"Aw, some kids chased me again," Arthur said, walking toward the fence where Ronald was standing.

"Who?" Ronald asked.

"It doesn't matter," Arthur answered.

"Well, then, why are you looking so sad?"

"I'm not sad. I was just thinking," Arthur explained.

"Come on out here on the courts and think a little about tennis." Ronald smiled as he spoke.

"Okay," Arthur said, and the day's lesson began.

The rest of the summer was a happy time for Arthur. He had learned a new sport, found a new friend, and though he was often chased from the courts, he was no longer lonely.

Even life with Mrs. Berry was beginning to seem possible. A few times Arthur even asked her to mend his shorts and once in a while he would suggest a favorite dish for dinner. Arthur was growing up.

"One of these days," he told his father, "I'm going to be as good a tennis player as Mr. Charity."

"Well, Arthur," his father replied, "I guess a man can do just about anything he wants, as long as he makes up his mind to do it and works hard enough at it. If you want to play tennis, I will help you all I can. Just don't ever let it get in the way of your education. There's more to life than baseball and tennis, you know."

Arthur wasn't sure that he agreed, but if his father said so, it was good enough for him.

That fall and winter Arthur worked hard in school and he did well. He wanted his father to be proud of him, and he wanted Mr. Charity to be proud of him, too.

Winter nights, lying awake in bed, he thought of the fun he had had the past summer, and he wondered if he would be playing tennis with Ronald Charity again during the summer to come.

Chapter 4

ARTHUR ASHE, CHAMPION

If learning the fundamental strokes of tennis had been difficult that first summer, improving those skills during the next two years required even more work and thought. Arthur's vacation days were planned as strictly as were his school days. Every week day from nine in the morning until noon, he played baseball with the boys at the park. Then he went over to the swimming pool for a dip before lunch. After lunch he had his practice period with Ronald Charity.

To hold Arthur's interest, Ronald set up goals for his pupil to reach by a certain time. One day he might say to Arthur, "Okay, let's work on the chop shot, so that by next week you can use it exactly right whenever you want to."

If he saw Arthur's racket hitting the ball too squarely, he would holler to the youngster to cut behind the ball more, and if he thought the ball was not coming over the net fast enough, he would tell him to get his body behind his swing. Once Arthur had learned a stroke thoroughly, Ronald would choose another shot for the boy to practice.

"That chop is much better. Now let's work on your volley, so that you can hit the ball without letting it bounce."

Two weeks later it would be something else, and something else after that. The method worked, and Arthur's game steadily improved. By the summer that Arthur was nine, no one even tried to chase him off the courts, and a few older people were happy to hit tennis balls with him.

On the days that were too hot to work out for more than short periods, Ronald would sit with Arthur and discuss school and tennis and what Arthur wanted to be when he grew up. By this time Arthur had decided on a future in baseball.

"There are lots of other things you could do, Arthur," Ronald would sometimes say, hoping to change his mind. "If you are so set on sports, you know, you might become a pretty good tennis player. Maybe you can even go to college and play for your college team. I bet you don't even know the kind of life you can have if you are a tennis player."

"I know you can play in matches," Arthur answered, "and you can play on school teams. What else can you do with tennis?"

"Well," Ronald explained, "you can travel all over the world. If you are good enough, you can play at Wimbledon in England and at Forest Hills up in New York, and maybe at places like Spain and Australia. You might even make the United States Davis Cup Team."

Without having to say it, they both knew the dream stopped there. Who had ever heard of a Negro playing on the United States Davis Cup Team?

Each year, near the end of summer, a tennis tournament was held in Brookfield Park. The competition had been set up mostly for the young people in Arthur's neighborhood. It wasn't Wimbledon, but it was one of the few contests around in which Negro boys and girls had an opportunity to test their skills against one another. Almost all of the tennis matches in Richmond were only for white people.

Arthur had never played in the tournament. He had been far too young and too small to play against the boys who usually entered it. But the summer that Arthur was nine, Ronald Charity decided his pupil should join the list of those who were playing. He explained to Arthur that he should be prepared for some disappointments because most of the boys he would be matched against would be much bigger and older than he was.

Arthur practiced harder than ever. "I'd like to give those fellas who used to chase me a good whipping on the courts," he thought, as he worked to improve his forehand and backhand, to serve harder, to hit a higher lob or a sharper and more angled volley. Ronald had never seen Arthur work so hard on his tennis as in those weeks.

Then, one afternoon before his practice period with Ronald, all of Arthur's dreams seemed to melt away.

It was the quiet part of the day and no one was around. Arthur decided to take his bicycle out for a spin. He hadn't had much chance to ride it recently, and it was great fun to glide along the smooth paths.

He pretended he was an ambulance driver, a mortorcycle policeman, a six-day bicycle racer, skidding into the wet grass and dragging his foot on the turns. Once he had made his tour of the park, he sped off to the tennis courts. Not a soul was in sight and the flat, hard surface of the courts seemed to be calling him. He rode as fast as he could, then coasted up toward the fence. He was almost there when the wheel of his bicycle caught in a rut, and down he went.

He hit the ground hard, and for a minute he just lay there, aching. It wasn't until he tried to get up that his eyes began to fill with tears. He couldn't turn his head. Now he was scared. Would he never be able to move his head again?

Slowly he pulled himself to his feet and started walking toward his house.

Mrs. Berry took one look at young Arthur and knew from the tears in his eyes and the funny way he was walking and holding his head that something was seriously wrong.

"What on earth is the matter, child?" she asked as she rushed to the door to meet him.

"I can't turn my head," Arthur answered, fighting to stop the tears.

"What happened?" Mother Berry demanded, putting her hand gently on his back and pulling him toward her.

"I was riding my bicycle over by the tennis courts and I fell," he told her.

It was easy to see that Arthur was in pain and that something was wrong with his neck. Mrs. Berry decided to call a doctor.

Arthur waited for the doctor to come, his mind whirling in fright. How could he play tennis or baseball if he couldn't turn his head? He thought of the tournament. His chance to win that was surely gone now.

The doctor's examination didn't take long, but it hurt. Arthur jumped each time the doctor felt the area around his neck and shoulders. No matter what happened, he had made up his mind not to cry.

"You are lucky, young fellow," the doctor said, closing his medical bag. "Looks like you are going to live."

"Will I be able to play baseball?" Arthur asked.

"Yes," the doctor laughed, "but first we are going to have to put you in the hospital for a while."

"The hospital?" Arthur said in surprise. "I have to play in a tennis tournament."

"Well, I'm afraid you may have to miss out on it," the doctor told him.

Arthur's collarbone had been broken in the fall, and only time could heal that.

An unhappy Arthur counted the days to the tournament as he lay in his hospital bed, and whenever Ronald Charity stopped in to see him, Arthur talked about nothing but playing in the competition.

"Look, Arthur," Ronald tried to comfort the boy, "if you don't play this year, you'll play next year. One year won't make that much difference."

Finally, Ronald asked the doctor if there was

any chance that Arthur would be well in time to play in the tennis matches.

"Collarbones usually take longer than a few weeks to heal," the doctor explained. "There's nothing anyone can do to speed up that process."

But as if by a miracle, Arthur got out of the hospital in only two weeks. His young body had healed quickly—sooner than anyone had thought it could—and he was back at Brookfield Park again, preparing for the tournament.

At first he had to go slowly, to get his shoulder and neck muscles in shape again. He knew he couldn't waste any time, for the matches were now only a week and a half away.

If anyone had asked Ronald Charity then what was the most striking thing about Arthur's tennis, he would have said, "Arthur's ability to learn a stroke almost as quickly as it is shown to him." Of course, Arthur didn't perfect a stroke that quickly, but Ronald was more and more surprised at the improvement Arthur made.

By the time the tournament began, Arthur was a ball of fire. He beat the first boy he played easily, and went on to win his next match as well. There was no question about it, the boys he was playing were much bigger and stronger than he was, but still Arthur kept on winning.

Then, one afternoon, a crowd gathered to watch young Mr. Arthur Ashe, Junior, play tennis. It was the final match of the tournament. Arthur fought all the way. He hit his strokes so hard that it almost seemed his thin body would go bouncing away after the ball. The boy Arthur was playing against was much bigger. He was also three years older than Arthur.

For nearly an hour the two raced around the Brookfield court, swatting the ball back and forth. When the match ended, Arthur was the winner!

He was Arthur Ashe, Champion Tennis Player of Brookfield Park, and he had a medal to prove it. Now, no one would ever chase him off the courts again.

Seeing Arthur play so well in competition, Ronald Charity knew that what he had been thinking for so long was right. Arthur needed more expert instruction than Ronald himself could offer. He had taught the boy everything he knew, and now Arthur's future had to be placed in the hands of a more professional coach, someone who could guide this tennis talent to the heights. Ronald knew just the man for the job.

At the first opportunity, Ronald called Doctor R. Walter Johnson, in Lynchburg, Virginia. In those days, as now, Doctor Johnson not only carried on a busy medical practice, but was an active official of the American Tennis Association, a group formed for Negro tennis players.

For years, Doctor Johnson had been fighting to

see that Negro boys and girls had as much of a chance as white boys and girls to rise to the top of the tennis world. It was under him that Althea Gibson, one of the finest women tennis players in history, had become the American woman national champion. And she had done it at a time when tennis officials were not eager to let Negroes play in their competitions. It was under Doctor Johnson that many other young tennis players were now advancing in the ranks. Doctor Johnson worked hard to help anyone who showed talent in the sport, and Ronald thought he would be the best man to help Arthur Ashe.

"I've got a very promising young boy down here," Ronald Charity told Doctor Johnson when he got him on the phone. "I think you ought to take a look at him."

"Well, if you think so, Ronald," Doctor Johnson answered. "What's his name?"

"Arthur Ashe. I can bring him down to Lynchburg whenever you like. When do you want to see him?"

As soon as he had watched Arthur play, Doctor Johnson recognized the boy's ability. But as he pointed out to both Arthur and his father, having a talent for something is only half the battle. You have to keep practicing and improving.

Each summer, Doctor Johnson would invite some of the better young tennis players to his home for two weeks during the American Tennis Association's Interscholastic Tournaments. Sometimes he would play host to as many as eighteen boys, keeping them at his own expense, providing them with expert coaching, and devoting every minute of his spare time to encouraging them. But he had never taken a boy as young as Arthur.

"He has good strokes, keeps his eye on the ball. That's good. He sees it when he hits it," Doctor Johnson told Ronald Charity. "He doesn't bend his knees enough, though, and his racket is much too heavy for him. When he swings it, he looks more like he's throwing himself at the ball than stroking it. A lighter racket will correct that, I think.

"If Arthur's father approves, I will invite Arthur to Lynchburg, where my son Robert and I can work with him."

It was a difficult decision for Arthur's father to make. He didn't like the idea of Arthur going away, even for two weeks. Wasn't Arthur much too young? What would Arthur's mother have thought about it? He decided to talk it over with Mrs. Berry and with Arthur's grandfather and grandmother, and finally with the minister of the church before giving his answer. All were agreed. It was a wonderful opportunity for Arthur, and even if it didn't turn out as well as everyone hoped, it could do him no harm.

Everyone felt that way but Arthur himself. At

nights he lay awake thinking over how different his life would be now. He liked tennis well enough, but he liked it because he enjoyed playing the game with his friends at the park and with Ronald Charity. Certainly tennis wasn't his whole life. How could he be sure he would like living with Doctor Johnson and his son for two weeks? They probably wouldn't let him play baseball at all. It was a big change for a nine-year-old boy to make, and Arthur wasn't at all certain that he wanted to make it.

Chapter 5

THE CHOICE

Doctor Johnson's home in Lynchburg would have been called grand by almost any standards. By the standards of Negroes who lived in the South, it was a palace. Large and handsome, it had its own tennis court in the back, and magnificent flower beds surrounded its clean, trim lawns. It was a thrilling place for just about every young person who was invited there—everyone except its newest visitor, Arthur Ashe.

In the first place, Arthur thought, Lynchburg was not nearly so clean and handsome a city as Richmond, and in the second place, he found it hard to believe that anyone could know more about tennis than Ronald Charity. In any event, being away from his home and his friends made Arthur unhappy. He liked to play when he wanted to play and to quit when he wanted to quit. At the Johnsons' it was just the opposite. His every move was planned, and practice seemed to him to last all day.

There was no doubt about it, the program at the Johnsons' was demanding, particularly for a nine-year-old boy. Every morning at 6:30 the youngsters were turned out of bed and sent off to the practice courts, where they worked out until breakfast. After breakfast they were permitted a half-hour rest period, and were then hurried back to the courts again. It was all work until nearly five o'clock in the afternoon. Those who weren't sweating it out on the courts were doing exercises, and those who weren't doing exercises were doing some job around the house.

Doctor Johnson's many flower beds, of which he was so fond, had to be kept up, the flowers watered and the beds weeded. And then there were hedges to be trimmed, grass to be cut, and the dog house, where Doctor Johnson kept his hunting dogs, to be cleaned.

What had once been a life of play for Arthur had been changed overnight into a round of hard work. Even in the evenings, which were supposed to be set aside for rest, Doctor Johnson often showed a tennis movie.

Arthur had trouble learning from his new tennis teachers. Until now, he had been taught only by Ronald Charity. Arthur respected and admired Ronald and felt it necessary to defend Ronald's methods. When the Johnsons asked Arthur to make changes in his game, Arthur openly refused.

Doctor Johnson was less patient with Arthur than his father, or Mrs. Berry, or Ronald Charity had been. The doctor believed in laying things on the line.

"If you can't do it our way, Arthur," he told the boy, "we have no choice but to send you back home. If you aren't here to improve your tennis, there's no reason for you to be here at all. If you are here to improve, then you have to listen to our suggestions and try to adopt our methods."

Arthur agreed, but he was slow to respond. Among the parts of Arthur's game that the Johnsons hoped to change was the way he gripped his racket. They thought a more modern grip would be better, particularly for such a young player. They tried to tell him that anyone who used the kind of grip that Ronald Charity had taught him had to have strong wrists. Once he started playing matches against players who could hit the ball harder and faster than he could, he would have trouble returning their shots if he didn't change.

"Most top tennis players today use an Eastern or a Western grip. With those grips your entire arm, instead of just your wrist, takes the pressure of a well hit ball," Robert Johnson explained.

The argument seemed true enough. Still, Arthur

kept on using the old grip. If the grip was good enough for Ronald Charity, it was good enough for Arthur.

"I like this grip. It feels comfortable to me. I'm used to it," Arthur argued.

Finally, he had his way about the grip. But there were other things to which the boy from Richmond refused to listen. For Robert Johnson, instruction periods with Arthur were hard work without much to show for it.

"Get your body around on those forehands! Turn your left hip to the net on them. Bend your knees! Don't stand so flat on your feet," Robert could be heard yelling to Arthur almost every day, but little of what he said showed in Arthur's play.

At last, Robert could stand it no longer. He went to his father and told the doctor how impossible the situation was:

"Dad," he said, "I think we are going to have to send Arthur back. He isn't following my instructions at all. To get him to change anything, to get him to give one ounce of effort even, is a real fight."

Doctor Johnson was used to such struggles. Even with his best pupils there was always a difficult period. He remembered Althea Gibson and the trouble he had getting her to practice and to learn certain new methods.

"It would be a pity to see a boy as talented as Arthur Ashe lose a chance to make something of himself, Robert," the doctor told his son. "He's the youngest boy we've ever worked with, and he's good. Maybe we had better try just a little harder before we give up."

Doctor Johnson decided to take another approach to "the Arthur Ashe problem." He sent for Arthur's father, and asked him to speak to his son.

As soon as Arthur caught a glimpse of the stern look on his father's face, he knew this visit wasn't for pleasure. Almost immediately Arthur decided to change the way he had been acting.

"Son," his father said sharply, "Mr. Charity sent you here because he believed Doctor Johnson could do more for you now than he could. Mr. Charity felt that he had reached the limit of his capacity, and he wanted you to have the benefit of being taught by others who know more about this game than he does. Now that's what he wants for you, and that's what we all want for you—if that's what you want for yourself. But you have to make up your own mind about that, and you have to decide now. Do you want to stay here, or do you want to go home?"

Arthur had never failed his father in his life. He hoped he never would, and he wasn't going to now.

43

"I want to stay," Arthur answered.

Arthur stayed and he worked hard. He didn't always appreciate the experience and he didn't always like what he had to do, but he did it anyway. Strangely enough, his grip stayed too. He was becoming so good with it that the Johnsons decided there would be no sense changing it.

Arthur found it difficult not being able to do things his own way and in his own time. Tennis, he was sure, could never be his whole life. He missed the freedom to run off with his friends for a dip in the swimming pool, or to play on the big park lawns near his house. Most of all, he missed playing baseball. How, he wondered, could anyone like Doctor Johnson eat, breathe, and sleep tennis? The library in the Johnson home held shelf after shelf of tennis books. Movies, books, talk—they were all about the one subject.

Arthur might not understand such devotion to tennis, but slowly he began to appreciate what the Johnsons were trying to do for him. At least, in return, he could try to learn as much as possible he decided.

"Arthur became one of my model pupils," Doctor Johnson later told a newspaper reporter, "after a while, anyway. He was a good student, too. He never showed any temper. Often when he missed an easy shot, he would smile, instead of slamming his racket down. He never felt sorry for him-self."

Both Arthur's attitude and his tennis began to show their good qualities. During the second week that Arthur spent in Lynchburg that first summer, he won two tournaments for young boys run by the American Tennis Association.

His hard work was beginning to pay off.

Chapter 6

GROWING PAINS

Arthur Ashe returned to Richmond fired with enthusiasm after his triumphs in Lynchburg. It was now almost impossible for the boys in Brookfield Park to beat him. Tennis had become a more important part of his young life.

The change in his son worried Arthur's father.

"I told you before," he said to Arthur, "that I would help you become a good tennis player, and I will. But I also said that your education came first. You get yourself a good education, Arthur, and then you can choose what you want to be."

Arthur promised to do his best, and he did. He had never minded doing his lessons. Class work came rather easily to him, and his grades were the best proof of it. He was proud of himself as a student.

When Johnny started going to school, Mrs. Berry ordered Arthur to help his younger brother.

"Why do I have to help him?" Arthur complained.

"Because you are older and that's what big brothers are for," Mother Berry told him. "Besides, you are a bright boy and you understand the school work Johnny has now. You should be glad to help him out."

"But how can I get my own school work done if I'm helping him? Nobody helps me," Arthur argued.

"You be quiet and help your little brother like I told you," Mother Berry commanded.

Arthur helped Johnny, but he didn't like it. Johnny always seemed to get his way about everything. "Mrs. Berry spoils him because he's the youngest, and because she's the only mother Johnny's ever known," Arthur thought. "Things would be different if my own mother were alive."

But things weren't quite as bad as Arthur had thought they would be. Johnny was a bright boy, and helping him proved to be almost no job at all.

School itself wasn't all work for Arthur, either. As he got older, it offered him one of his first big opportunities to do what he liked best—play baseball. He decided that the fun of playing on a team and winning was much greater than the lonely glory of a victory in tennis.

Arthur was small for his age and he couldn't hit

very hard, and that in itself was a problem. Still, his coaches liked him. He was eager and he moved well. He had quick hands and a strong arm, and he never gave up, no matter how far behind his team was.

One morning when the regular pitcher on Arthur's grade school team failed to show up for practice, Arthur's coach, Maxy Robinson, handed Arthur the ball.

"Art," the coach called to him, "suppose you pitch batting practice this morning."

Arthur had played second base, but that morning marked the end of his fielding career. He showed that he could help the team more as a pitcher.

Arthur was delighted. He began to read all he could about pitching greats like Whitey Ford, Don Newcombe, Warren Spahn, and the wonderful Satchel Paige.

He had never really had any tennis heroes. "Althea Gibson didn't light any fires in me," he said later. "I guess a boy needs men heroes."

Arthur did well in school and he did well on the baseball team, too. In fact he did so well in grade school baseball that he could hardly wait to try out for the junior high school team when the time came. Arthur tried out for both the baseball team and the tennis team his first year in junior high, and to his great surprise he made both. But there was a difference. He had to work for the honor of being a member of the school baseball team—making the tennis team was easy. As a matter of fact, he never had to come to tennis team practice. He simply appeared for matches and defeated the boys who played against him.

Baseball was another story. Every afternoon he arrived on time for the team workout and gave the practice everything he had, and every game he sat on the bench, waiting for a chance to prove himself on the mound. It seemed as though his chance would never come. Then, one afternoon, it happened.

The team was playing a Petersburg, Virginia, junior high school. It was the top of the sixth, and the Richmond team was in trouble.

"If Richmond ever needed a relief pitcher, it's now," Arthur thought to himself.

He was so wrapped up in the game, he almost failed to notice his coach signaling him to warm up. By the time he reached the mound, he was beginning to feel nervous. He was damp with sweat—sweat that he knew, came more from being scared than from the heat. All too soon he had made his last practice pitch and was watching the first Petersburg batter walk to the plate, swinging his bat with a sharp and threatening snap. Arthur watched his catcher's signals, paused, kept his eye on the spot he was aiming for, and threw.

50

"Strike one," the umpire yelled.

The batter hit Arthur's second pitch foul, and missed the third completely.

"Strike three," the umpire yelled. Arthur had gotten the first man out—and then the second—and was really throwing well as he sent the third Petersburg batter down swinging to retire the side. He hadn't allowed a single player to reach base safely. In the seventh inning, Arthur's coach called on another relief pitcher and Arthur went back to the bench.

Being pulled out of the game after having done so well angered the boy. He wouldn't have minded being taken out if he had done a bad job. Even the other guys on the team didn't understand it, and told him so after the game was over and they were on their way home.

"Next time I'm really going to show that coach how well I can pitch," he said to himself that night. "And I'm going to improve my hitting, too, even if I have to work on it every day after school and every Saturday and forget about tennis."

Arthur might have been perfectly willing to "forget about tennis," but there were others who were not going to let him. And these people had the authority to back up their decisions.

The next morning Arthur had hardly reached his home room and prepared his books for class when his teacher told him that the principal wanted to see him.

"Art," the principal said when he entered the office, "you've pitched your last baseball game."

"What . . . what do you mean, sir?" Arthur asked, surprised.

"I mean you've had it," the principal told him. "You are just too fine a tennis player. That's where you belong, in tennis, and to be sure that you make the most of your talents, I'm kicking you off the ball team."

Arthur was never one to argue a point with his superiors. He knew it would do no good to argue with the principal, anyway. He had no choice but to accept the principal's order, but he was far from happy about it. And it didn't make him any more fond of the sport he sometimes seemed "condemned" to play.

Getting kicked off the baseball team wasn't the only surprise in store for Arthur. In 1956, six years after his first wife's death, Mr. Ashe married again. His new wife's name was Lorraine Kimbrough. She and Mr. Ashe had been seeing each other for months before they decided to marry. Arthur knew of it and did not object to the marriage when his father told him of his plans. Perhaps Arthur found the decision easy to accept because he was so busy with his own problems.

Besides, she did not meddle in his affairs. She was quiet and when she spoke to him her voice was always soft. She seemed to understand how he felt, and she was a good cook, too. So the Ashes became a family of five—the boys, their father, Mrs. Berry, and the new Mrs. Ashe.

Most of the boys at Arthur's school preferred contact sports, like football and basketball, to the more "refined" sport of tennis. In fact, many of them considered tennis a "sissy" game. They didn't know how much physical strength it took to play for hours in the hot sun, running at top speed around the court, with almost no opportunity to rest. What they knew about tennis was little more than "patty cake"—punching at a tennis ball with a worn out racket. They usually played this game in the street, without a net, when there was nothing else to do.

Arthur's tennis skill meant little to them, and it began to rub them the wrong way to hear teachers openly praise Arthur for doing so well, both in the class room and on the courts. To his fellow students, Arthur Ashe was just too much of a good thing.

Actually Arthur did play some basketball. He went out for track, too. He had even hoped to play football, but his father refused to sign the permission slip. Arthur was too slender for a sport as rough as football. Still, the other students were jealous because Arthur was such a favorite with the teachers, and they began to make his life miserable. They swiped his books, poured ink on his home work, and tore his clothes. They shoved him around and teased him about how strict his father was and about how early he had to be home at night. If he had a little extra time and hung around the crowd at school, they would make fun of him.

"Hey, Ashe, you'd better get on home before you are late and your daddy k-i-i-l-l-s-s you."

The way the boys treated Arthur hurt him badly, but he tried not to show his feelings. They just didn't understand. They couldn't appreciate the quiet young man's need to learn and his capacity to do so.

Joey Kennedy understood, though. Joey's father was the high school band director, and Arthur and Joey became close friends. Joey, too, did well in school, and both boys played in the band. Arthur played the trumpet.

In music, Arthur considered Joey a genius, and in science class, the two boys frequently tried to see who could finish a problem first.

Arthur noticed one difference between himself and Joey. Joey was never satisfied with anything he did until it was just the way he wanted it or just the way it should be. Arthur knew this was not true of himself. Even though he might practice and work at a thing, Arthur tended to take the results in an easy going manner. He usually enjoyed playing tennis, and he liked getting good grades in school, but he seldom worked at anything with a burning desire.

"If you are the best, why that's one thing. But if you aren't, you don't have to try to be better than someone who is. I believe in being myself, and I don't have to be better than anybody to be happy," Arthur told Joey as they left school one afternoon.

Arthur could prove he meant it. He remembered the time he had tried out for a part in the school play and had heard a teacher remark that another boy had read the part better than he had, but would not get the part because his parents couldn't afford to buy him a new suit for the play.

Arthur had gone home that night and asked his father if he could lend the boy one of his suits. The boy got the suit and the part, and Arthur was happier than if he had won the part himself.

Although Arthur liked to win when he played tennis, he never felt that he had to "break his neck," the way some of his friends did. Every time he watched Joey work and work to perfect some little thing, Arthur couldn't help but wonder about himself and his future in tennis. Would he have to be like Joey? Could he be?

Chapter 7

A MATTER OF COLOR

The insulting remarks of his school mates were not the only problem Arthur had to face in Richmond. By this time he had learned to play tennis too well to get much of a game from anyone who played at Brookfield Park.

One afternoon, hoping to find better players in one of the other areas of town, Arthur set off for Grant Park, which had been set aside for the use of Richmond's white citizens. He went in search of a good game of tennis, but he found something very different.

As soon as one of the park officials spotted the lean Negro boy standing around waiting for a turn on the courts, he came over to Arthur. The man never raised his voice, but what he said was quite simple and to the point:

"You can't play here. You have to be white to play here. You'd better go back to Brookfield Park before you get in trouble."

Arthur didn't bother to argue. He was old enough to know better. But knowing better didn't make it any less bitter a pill to swallow. It troubled him as he made his way home that afternoon, and it continued to bother him for days afterward. For the first time, he felt he really understood what being born a Negro meant. It was a list of things, a list that Arthur recited to himself in anger.

"It means you are allowed to ride only in the back of the bus, even if you have to stand, even though there are empty seats in the front where the white people sit.

"It means that you aren't permitted to sit down at the counter in the soda fountains down town or to buy from the candy stands, no matter how thirsty or hungry you are.

"It means that you have to sit in the 'Crow's nest,' way up in the balcony, at the local movie theaters. That is, if the manager even lets you into his theater at all.

"It means that you are one of the people who lives in that other part of town and goes to those other schools and plays in those other parks on the other side of the tracks."

The new feeling of being a Negro even began to affect Arthur's tennis. He was careful about entering tournaments, particularly in southern states. Doctor Johnson suggested that Arthur enter one of the big contests for boys under sixteen years of age. It was to be held in Florida, and Arthur didn't know if he should go.

There had been a number of fights between whites and Negroes in Florida that year. The fights had been so terrible that some of Arthur's teachers felt they should try to persuade him not to go. They thought that he was too young to have to face the problems that might arise.

"Look, Dad," Arthur said to his father one evening after they had finished supper, "perhaps I shouldn't go. I don't want to disappoint Doctor Johnson, but maybe it isn't a good idea."

"Arthur," Mr. Ashe spoke sharply, "there's no reason why you can't go to Florida. I've gone several times myself. The people always treated me well enough. But if you go down there to make trouble or to do things you shouldn't, then you won't get along all right. Just do as Doctor Johnson tells you, boy."

Arthur took his father's advice and went to Florida. He played well too, and no one yelled at him, no one insulted him.

When he returned home, Arthur told his father of his experience and thanked him for encouraging him to go. But both of them knew why Arthur was received so well in Florida, and neither of them could bear to say that reason out loud. It was because Arthur had remembered that he was a Negro and that as a Negro he had to keep his "place"—a very special place, outside the white world.

Much later, Arthur played in Fort Worth, Texas. It was one of the first tournaments in Texas that allowed whites and Negroes to compete against each other. Arthur told a newspaper reporter: "The real southern accent still frightens me." And he didn't think it was funny the way "colored employees at the club stared" at him as though he just didn't belong. Some of the Negro help actually thought he was "a waiter who had dressed up and tried to sneak in" to the party being held there.

If those experiences were less than pleasant, however, they were nothing compared to the one that occurred one evening after a tournament in Charlottesville, Virginia.

To the white tennis players, Arthur was just one of the gang. He liked them and they liked him. He even allowed some of them to call him "Shadow" because he "was the darkest thing in sight," as he himself put it. He got along well with everyone, even with white players born and raised in the South, such as Butch Newman of Texas, who was to become a good friend. It seemed only natural when the boys decided to go to the movies one evening that they invite Arthur.

"I don't think so," was Arthur's reply. "Thanks anyway."

"Why not? Come on, it will be fun," they urged.

"I think I'd better write a letter to my dad," Arthur answered.

"What's the matter? You got a big date on or something? You holding out on us?" they joked with him.

Still, Arthur hung back. Finally, one of them walked over to him and asked quietly if something was wrong. Had he received bad news from home? Or had one of them insulted him in any way?

"Look," Arthur burst out at last, "there's no sense my going with you. I know they won't let me sit where you sit even if they let me in, and I doubt if they will let me in."

"Why, for gosh sakes?" one of the boys asked.

"Because I'm a Negro."

The Northerners in the party were surprised. "Are you kidding?" they exclaimed.

"No, I'm not kidding," Arthur assured them.

"Look," one of the southern boys suggested, "let's try. What can they do if you go with us in a group?"

Arthur knew well enough what "they" could do, but he let himself be convinced that it might be different this time. Hadn't he been in Florida? He had had no trouble there. He went around with white tennis players all the time.

The scene at the movie theater was short but not sweet. The whole gang lined up at the ticket window, and one by one stepped forward and bought their tickets—until Arthur's turn came.

"Sorry, we are all sold out," the lady at the ticket window said to Arthur.

"Now wait a minute," one of the boys protested.

"Yeah, how come?" another argued.

It was almost as though the entire scene had been written down in advance. The next one to speak was the manager of the theater. He seemed to step out of nowhere, coming quickly toward Arthur.

"You know what we mean. We are all sold out, like we told you," he said. "The rest of you get on inside and don't start any trouble or you'll be sorry."

"Nothing doing," one of the boys replied. "We go together or not at all."

"If he can't go in, lady, we aren't going in," the others said flatly.

She simply looked at them and gave them back their money.

All the way home from the theater Arthur and his friends tried to make jokes about people who take sides against others because of their religion or color or because their noses are crooked or their eyes are straight. They laughed at how stupid it was, but all the jokes didn't hide the hurt that was inside each of them for having seen this kind of thing happen, and none felt that hurt more sharply than Arthur Ashe.

Arthur Ashe, Junior, at age two. Home was a happy place to Arthur in those days, before his mother died and before anyone made him feel different because of the color of his skin.

Eight-year-old Arthur (right) poses with Mrs. Berry and brother Johnny on the steps of their home in Richmond.

His first championship: Arthur (center) had to beat all the older and bigger boys in Brookfield Park to win this tournament.

More matches, more trophies: An unusual talent for the game begins to show itself as Arthur competes against other young Negroes.

Doctor Walter Johnson (left) and Arthur talk over old times. "Arthur...was a good student.... He never showed any temper.... He never felt sorry for himself," the doctor later told newspaper reporters. But both he and Arthur well knew that in the beginning the going wasn't at all easy.

Moving up: Arthur joins some other junior players after an Eastern Lawn Tennis Association tournament. The summers with Doctor Johnson are now paying off, and Arthur is advancing in the Eastern ranks.

As the years go by the trophies pile up: Arthur's father and stepmother pose with some of the spoils of victory.

Arthur, 17, shakes the hand of Richard Hudlin (right), the man who brings him to St. Louis, Missouri so that he will have a chance to play tennis even during the winter.

Arthur and his buddies at U.C.L.A.: (left to right)
Charles Pasarell, Arthur, coach J. D. Morgan, Dave
Reed, and Dave Sanderlin. For coach Morgan it is an
important tennis team. For Arthur it is the start of a
whole new life, and Morgan is a powerful influence in it.

In 1963 Arthur goes to Wimbledon. It is his first trip
abroad. "I felt a little lost . . . ," he tells newsmen afterward. "Imagine thirty thousand people watching your
every move, and you realizing that you are just a speck
of dust among the greatest."

Arthur discusses court strategy with his first and only tennis hero Pancho Gonzales (left) and Luis Ayala (right). Says Arthur: "Gonzales is the nearest thing to me in the color of his skin, and he is the greatest tennis player in the world."

Arthur hits an underspin backhand volley in a moment of triumph at the Eastern Grass Courts Championship in 1964. He gives his shots everything he's got and marches through such tough competition as Dennis Ralston, Gene Scott, and Clark Graebner to win the tournament.

"I hope I can prove to be the exception to the rule that 'good guys' always finish last," Arthur jokes, as United States Lawn Tennis Association President James Dickey presents him with the Johnston Sportsmanship Award —considered to be this country's highest tennis honor.

The U.S. Davis Cup Team of 1965: (left to right) E. Victor Seixas (then captain), Chuck McKinley, Dennis Ralston, Marty Riessen, Clark Graebner, Arthur (the first Negro ever to play on a U.S. Davis Cup team), Frank Froehling, Charles Pasarell, and coach Ed Faulkner, at the Challenge Round matches in Cleveland in September.

Moment of moments: Putting his strokes together in unbeatable combinations, Arthur (in background) keeps Osuna on the run in the interzone Davis Cup matches at Dallas later that same year. Again and again the Mexican is caught flat-footed, lunging at and missing impossible passing shots.

Time out from tennis: Arthur jokes with friend and fellow player Carole Graebner during a tournament tour to Australia in 1966.

With the team score at 2–1 in favor of the United States and one more match point needed to win, Arthur serves to Antonio Palafox to begin the fourth match of the Davis Cup series against Mexico, in 1965.

At the U.S. National Championship in 1965, Arthur overpowers Roy Emerson (right) 13–11, 6–4, 10–12, 6–2. Emerson's drawn, hollow-faced appearance tells the whole story of the match.

An important moment: Mayor Morrill Crowe presents Arthur with a copy of the Richmond City Council's resolution proclaiming February 4, 1966 as "Arthur Ashe Day."

Arthur, then ranked No. 2 in the country, shows his concern for kids by participating in a tennis clinic. Here he shows his form to a group of youngsters in Washington, D. C.

Arthur falls to grass attempting shot against Jim McManus in the National Singles Championship at Longwood Cricket Club, August 1968. He went on to defeat Bob Lutz in the final and became the first Negro ever to win a U. S. Men's tennis championship.

Now the big one—the U.S. Open Tennis Championship, the winner to be declared the No. 1 player in the world. Here Arthur, still giving it everything he has, lunges for a shot during an early round.

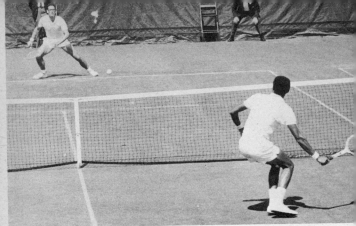

Arthur slaps a shot to his Davis Cup teammate, Clark Graebner, during their U.S. Open Tennis Championship semi-final match, September 8, 1968. The winner will meet Tom Okker of the Netherlands in the finals.

Lt. Arthur Ashe smashes a return to "the Dutchman," Tom Okker, during their heroic struggle for ranking as the world's best player. In a stirring five-set match, Arthur prevails and wins the first U.S. Open Championship ever conducted in this country.

Arthur holds up his trophy after defeating his gallant
opponent, Tom Okker, on September 9, 1968 for the
men's singles title in the U.S. Open Tennis Championship
at Forest Hills Stadium, New York.

The supreme moment for father and champion. Arthur
Ashe, Sr. gives way to tears as he embraces his victorious
son after the Okker match. It had been a long road from
the tennis courts in a Richmond, Virginia park to the
acclaim and adulation at Forest Hills, the mecca of world
tennis.

Arthur, again a member of the Davis Cup Team, practices his forehand shot during a warmup session in preparation for the challenge round matches with Australia, holder of the Cup.

The newly-crowned U.S. Open Champion, makes a forehand return from the baseline in his match against Roy Ruffels of Australia, December 1968, at the Memorial Drive Courts, Adelaide, South Australia. Arthur scored the second point for the U.S. forces, which swept to victory by 4 matches to 1.

The victorious Davis Cup Squad stands behind the famous trophy, now to be returned to the United States for the first time in five years. Arthur's winning smile expresses his pride in having reached this climax to a most remarkable year.

Chapter 8

THE START OF SOMETHING BIG

Arthur Ashe was growing up. He was tall for his age now. He was as slender as he had been at ten, but he had shot up to over six feet in height. With long legs that could cover the court in easy strides and long arms that could reach out for the ball and whip it back over the net, Arthur was a fourteen-year-old who had a chance to become a champion.

During the last two summers he had stayed an entire month with Doctor Johnson, working on his game. He had skipped rope to build his strength and he had practiced the difficult shots longer than even Doctor Johnson thought he should.

And Arthur had found a hero, a tennis player he really wanted to be like—Pancho Gonzales, champion tennis player of the world. Pancho ruled the court with his power and his brilliant shots. Arthur watched him in action when a group of professional players visited Richmond on a tour.

Never had he seen such strokes, such a will to win.

"He is the nearest thing to me in the color of his skin, and he is the greatest tennis player in the world," Arthur explained. In magazines and books he read about Pancho's boyhood in Los Angeles, about the trouble Pancho had had because of the Mexican blood that separated him from the "white" players on the California courts.

"You might be almost as good as Gonzales some day," a friend remarked to Arthur as they watched the great professional play.

"You must be crazy, man," Arthur answered.

Arthur had shown such improvement that Doctor Johnson decided to step up the pace of his tennis. He entered the boy in tournaments up and down the East Coast, encouraging Arthur as he went to each one: "You can win. Go out there and do your best."

Arthur did win, not just local and state contests, but tournaments held by the United States Lawn Tennis Association. He was beginning to play at a level that would soon match him against the best in the nation. The hope that had begun the day Ronald Charity had shown him how to hold a racket was becoming real for a young man not quite fifteen who could go anywhere and play against the best tennis players of his age.

In 1958, Arthur's tournament record was so

good that he earned himself national ranking in the Lawn Tennis Association ratings. In fact, this almost unknown Negro boy was placed Number 5—the fifth best player in the United States under the age of fifteen!

Arthur's national ranking was more than anyone had hoped for. The name Ashe was becoming known in tennis circles across the country. His skill, in fact, was the subject of a conversation between two men sitting in an office in St. Louis, Missouri.

The office was that of Washington University's Director of Athletics, Harry Burrus, and Burrus was entertaining an old friend of his named Richard Hudlin, a high school history teacher.

Richard Hudlin had played tennis himself for fifty years, and his own life had been greatly influenced by the game. Now, no longer an active player, he found real satisfaction in helping young would-be champions. His visit to Doctor Burrus's office had been brought about by just such an interest. He was looking for a job for one of the players he was helping through college.

"If you really want to help a tennis player," Doctor Burrus said, after listening to his friend, "you ought to help a player from Richmond I've heard something about—young Arthur Ashe."

Hudlin admitted that he had heard about Arthur, but he had not kept close track of him.

"However," the school teacher promised, "if he's as good as you say he is, I want to help him all I can."

"See if you can get him to come to school here," Doctor Burrus said. "The university might even help pay his way."

"Is he old enough for college?"

"Darned if I know. He should be, judging by the players he's beaten. Let's find out."

Hudlin learned that Arthur was playing in a tournament at Hampton Institute in Virginia and would be difficult to reach. He decided to talk to Doctor Johnson, who told him Arthur was only in his junior year in high school. Surprised, Hudlin returned to Harry Burrus for another talk, and Burrus suggested that they bring Arthur out anyway.

"We can keep him here for a year and train him over the winter. Let's see how well he does."

Richard Hudlin explained the plans that he and Harry Burrus had for Arthur to Mr. Ashe, but Arthur's father wasn't at all sure he liked the idea of his son going so far away for so long a time. He had raised his boys without the help of a mother and he knew he was very close to them. He didn't want to be separated from Arthur if it wasn't necessary.

"I don't know, Mr. Hudlin. Arthur is away practically every summer and he's getting to be a young man. What little free time we have, I like to spend with my boy."

"I know how you must feel," Hudlin said, "but Arthur's doing so well that Doctor Burrus and I think one winter of indoor tennis might be very good for his game. It could be just what he needs to move up in the rankings."

"How much will it cost?" Mr. Ashe asked. Raising a young boy to be a tournament tennis player, he had discovered, was an expensive business. In an average season, a young tournament player spent about $80 for shirts, $72 for shorts, $60 for socks, $150 for tennis shoes, and at least $750 for rackets and strings.

"It won't cost anything," Richard Hudlin assured him. "We plan to give Arthur room and board."

Mr. Ashe thanked Hudlin for being so generous. There were, he explained, many things to consider. He wanted time to think the matter over before giving his answer.

If it had been difficult to decide whether or not to let Arthur go to Lynchburg for two weeks when he was nine years old, it seemed ten times harder to decide whether or not to let Arthur go to St. Louis for an entire school year now that he was in his teens. Mr. Ashe thought it best to talk the problem over with Doctor Johnson.

He knew only too well that his son was being

made fun of by his school mates in Richmond, even though Arthur seldom spoke of it. Mr. Ashe was upset, too, because the white people of Richmond refused to accept Arthur as a tennis player.

The first time Arthur had been asked to leave Grant Park had not been the last. Again he had walked over to the white man's play area in search of someone new to play against. Again he had been told to leave.

Also, members of the West Side Tennis Club in Forest Hills, New York, had written to Sam Woods, of Richmond's Department of Recreation, asking that Arthur be chosen as a member of Richmond's five-man team. This team was to play matches against the New York club. But the request had been turned down.

Arthur couldn't believe he wasn't going to be allowed to be on the Richmond team.

"Just pay no attention," his father told him. "You are going to have to face a lot of things in your life that are not pleasant and do not seem fair. Just keep going, keep trying to play better, keep trying to do whatever you want to do. Then, one day, people will respect you."

"But what's wrong with me playing tennis with them?" Arthur demanded.

His father had no answer.

Mr. Ashe had been very unhappy when he had

heard that the Richmond Recreation Department had turned down the request from the West Side Tennis Club. Without mentioning his feelings to anyone, he went straight to Sam Woods and asked for an explanation.

Woods' answer was firm. "I think it best that Arthur not try to take part in any of our tennis events," he told him.

"I'm sorry you feel that way about it, Mr. Woods," Mr. Ashe answered, "because one day you are all going to have to look up to my son."

St. Louis, Richard Hudlin told Mr. Ashe, was not like Richmond. In Missouri there was no color line to worry about when it came to sports. Arthur could get all the competition he wanted and needed.

"Perhaps Arthur *should* go to St. Louis," Mr. Ashe decided, as he thought over the offer.

Arthur's father wasn't the only one who had decided Arthur should go. So had Doctor Johnson.

"You are still developing," he explained to Arthur. "I know that you've worked hard and that you've learned a great deal. You've done well, and you will soon do better. Right now you need competition all year long. The season is too short here in Virginia and there just isn't any other place for you to play. In St. Louis you will have indoor courts and an opportunity to play winter tennis. You should go."

The only one who was completely opposed was Arthur himself. He still remembered that first unhappy summer in Lynchburg, and while he had to admit that it was all for his own good, he didn't want to experience the same feelings again.

He realized that what the Johnsons were doing in Lynchburg gave Negro boys their best chance to play serious tennis. He remembered talking to some of the young white players, and many of them had told him they paid as much as ten or fifteen dollars an hour for their tennis lessons. Arthur knew that if he had had to pay to learn the game, he would never have learned it at all.

Still, Arthur did not want to go to St. Louis. Opportunities existed in Richmond, and whatever problems he might have there, it was his home. His family was there, his friends were there, and he felt that he could be happier there than anywhere else.

If he stayed in Richmond, Arthur knew he could work with his father in the landscaping business Mr. Ashe was developing in his free time. Arthur was never paid for helping out, but his father gave him enough money to buy whatever he needed. Besides, Arthur liked helping his father.

And then there was the discipline that his tennis career demanded. He accepted the hard work and the practice schedules in the warm weather months, but he didn't think he could stand that kind of life the whole year round.

Arthur didn't want to leave. His father, Doctor Johnson, and Ronald Charity thought he should. The three men he respected most in the world were telling him to go. Whether he wanted to or not, he didn't really have a choice.

In the end, Arthur did what was asked of him, just as he had always done. In September 1960, he arrived in St. Louis by bus.

Richard Hudlin and his wife, Jane, did all they could to make Arthur comfortable. Mrs. Hudlin was a nurse, and she had both sympathy and patience for Arthur's problems. The Hudlins found Arthur a very shy young man, not at all given to easy conversation. Arthur found Richard Hudlin to be much the same sort of no-nonsense coach that Doctor Johnson had been.

"Bedtime is eleven o'clock," Hudlin announced, "and that includes Friday and Saturday nights."

"But that's silly," Arthur protested. "I'm a senior in high school and I don't want to go to bed at eleven o'clock, especially on Saturdays."

Richard Hudlin was all business. "You came here to play tennis. That's what you are going to do—including going to bed at eleven!"

Arthur knew that he could not just pack up and go home. It wasn't only Mr. and Mrs. Hudlin whose feelings he would hurt. There were Doctor

Johnson and Ronald Charity, not to mention Arthur's own father. They all had faith in him. They all had helped him and encouraged him. They all were counting on him to do well.

Down deep inside, Arthur argued that this was *his* life, not someone else's. A hundred years later, no one was going to know or care one way or the other. He didn't want tennis to be his whole life. He wanted to have some time to date girls, go to parties and dances, take in a late movie, and sleep late on Saturday mornings. Why did his family and his friends want him to give up everything for tennis?

"Big deal!" Arthur thought. It was his brother Johnny who always had fun. Johnny was five years younger, but he was already bigger than Arthur. Johnny was the one who won all the medals in swimming, and who was the fine baseball player. He had even made both the basketball and football teams at school. "I don't even know anyone in St. Louis—not one person," Arthur said to himself. "All my friends are in Richmond."

But Arthur stuck it out in St. Louis, and as winter came he found himself practicing as much as three to five hours a day on an indoor court. It was a lonely battle with himself and the tennis ball, but it was rewarding.

That year Arthur entered the 1960-61 U. S. Lawn Tennis Association's Junior Singles Indoor

Tournament, and astonished the tennis world by winning the title. He was now the best tennis player under nineteen years of age in the whole nation—at least on an indoor court.

Arthur was happy, but a greater joy lay ahead. During an Orange Bowl tournament in Miami, Florida, at Christmas time, Arthur was permitted to make a day trip to Richmond. It was a brief but pleasant visit with his family and friends, and it included a very special surprise.

At seven o'clock in the evening the phone rang. The man on the other end of the line said he was J. D. Morgan, director of athletics and tennis coach at the University of California at Los Angeles. Could he speak with Arthur?

Arthur jumped to the phone.

"How would you like to come to U.C.L.A.— with our help in paying your way—and play tennis for us?" the voice asked.

"Would I? That's like asking a baseball player in the minor leagues if he wants to play for the Yankees," Arthur replied.

During the next ten minutes, Mr. Morgan filled Arthur in on the details.

"I hope you aren't kidding me, Arthur," Morgan teased, as the two ended their conversation. "You *are* going to join us, aren't you?"

"Don't worry," Arthur answered eagerly, "nothing could keep me away!"

Chapter 9

LEARNING AND WINNING

U.C.L.A.! The University of California at Los Angeles. One of the Big Three of the West Coast. The college whose tennis team was almost a Davis Cup group in itself.

What boy from Richmond whose skin color had kept him in the back seat of the bus could ever have imagined such an invitation?

Strange as it seemed to Arthur, the truth was stranger. J. D. Morgan, the U.C.L.A. tennis coach, had first seen Arthur play when he was fifteen years old. Arthur was playing in a tournament in Michigan. Morgan thought then that the boy had great possibilities. Quietly, by telephone, he began to discuss with Doctor Johnson the chance of Arthur's going to U.C.L.A. when the time came. Doctor Johnson had never hinted to Arthur by so much as a word what might be in store. Better to have it come as a complete surprise than to risk any chance of a big disappointment.

Now it had all come true.

That summer, before Arthur packed his bags to travel to the West Coast, he played some of his finest tennis in the junior divisions. By September he not only held the U.S.L.T.A. National Interscholastic Outdoor Championship, but, because of his record, he had been named to the Junior Davis Cup Team. It was a happy young man, filled with confidence, who made his way from Virginia to California in the fall of 1961.

To Arthur U.C.L.A. meant many things. He knew the university had a high rating as a place of learning and that as a tennis school it had few peers. He also knew that J. D. Morgan had won more National Collegiate Athletic Association titles than any other coach.

As Arthur put it, "The climate was good and the tennis was year-round if you wanted it to be."

But as it turned out, U.C.L.A. offered Arthur more than he had either hoped or bargained for. It brought him both freedom and challenge. For the first time in his life, there was no one to tell him what to do. Of course, he had to attend classes, get good grades, and play tennis and play it well. But it was up to him to decide how to manage all this. There was no one standing over him, pushing him, telling him what and when to eat, when he could go to the movies, and what time to go to bed. For the first time in his life, Arthur was on his own—and he loved it.

His social life was a full one, including going to dances, dating girls, and going to movies and sports events with some of his tennis team mates. Not a soul at U.C.L.A. was jealous because Arthur did well in his studies. In fact, plenty of students did better than Arthur. And no one was bothered by the fact that he played tennis well. After all, that was one of the reasons he was there.

Curiously enough, it was tennis, rather than his studies, that gave Arthur his greatest challenge at U.C.L.A. When Ken Rosewall of Australia, one of the best tennis players in the world, had moved into the professional ranks and played Pancho Gonzales, Rosewall had said it was like being "thrown to the lions," so much more fierce and sharp was the type of play. Now Arthur Ashe, like a baseball player who moves from one league up to a higher one, was discovering that he, too, had much to learn about the sport in which he had already gone so far.

Arthur also discovered that his attitude toward tennis was changing. Before, he had always felt he was playing for somebody else—for his father, or Doctor Johnson, or Richard Hudlin, or Ronald Charity. At U.C.L.A. Arthur realized he was playing for himself, and he began to gain some understanding of his talent. He finally had to admit that those who had helped him had been right.

"I really have something here," he told himself aloud one day during a practice period. "I really have something."

Arthur was made the Number 3 player on the U.C.L.A. team. Only Charles Pasarell and Dave Reed were ranked ahead of him. Pasarell was National Junior Champion, and Reed held the junior title for Southern California. The team worked well together. They had to. Their coach, J. D. Morgan, would have stood for nothing less. Morgan was tough. The handsome, sandy-haired man worked Arthur harder than he had ever had to work in his life.

Discipline, in fact, was no problem for the U.C.L.A. tennis coach. This was not because his boys were more serious than most, but because Morgan was a man who commanded his players' respect. He would stand for no bursts of temper. As most members of his team soon realized, he could deal out a tongue lashing that would make bigger men than Arthur Ashe run for cover.

Arthur admired J. D. Morgan and he worked hard for the U.C.L.A. coach. Most of Arthur's practice periods were devoted to sharpening an already large number of strokes. He also had to learn to keep his mind more on the game.

"I try to feel easy on the court," Arthur told one reporter who questioned him about his style. "The ideal attitude is to be loose in body and tight in mind. I don't have much trouble with the physical bit. I guess I'm naturally fairly loose. But I can't always keep my mind firmly fixed on the game."

To keep one's mind firmly on the game in serious tennis is often half the battle. A player who lets up in an important match may quickly find himself in a hole that he just can't fight his way out of. It was necessary for Arthur to learn to think tennis, and only tennis, while he was on the court.

Coming into the stiffer competition of big college tennis, Arthur often found himself losing, and Morgan never hesitated to bawl Arthur out when he thought the young man deserved it.

By September, 1962, his second year at U.C.L.A., Arthur had played the entire eastern grass court circuit. At the turn of the year, he found himself facing his team mate, Dave Reed, in the Southern California Intercollegiate Men's Singles.

Arthur was too much for the man who ranked just above him on the U.C.L.A. team. All through the match, Arthur drove the ball deep and hard on his returns keeping Reed back at the base line, unable to come to the net to handle Arthur's soft, short drop shots. By mixing up his shots so well, Arthur won the match in straight sets, 6–3, 6–3.

His successes in matches against other colleges moved Arthur to the Number 2 position on the U.C.L.A. team, one spot behind his good friend and room mate, Charles Pasarell. Arthur's opportunities in the world of tennis suddenly seemed to be without end.

Chapter 10

THE TEST

As the summer of 1963 approached, twenty-year-old Arthur Ashe was definitely on the move. His first stop would be Wimbledon, England, for one of the world's great tournaments. Now the true depths of his courage and skill would be tested.

Of course, he didn't expect to be the champion, and he wasn't. "I felt a little lost," he said of the experience on the famous old courts. "Imagine thirty thousand people watching your every move, and you realizing that you are just a speck of dust among the greatest."

In spite of Arthur's defeat by America's Number 1 player, Chuck McKinley, Wimbledon gave the young man from Richmond some valuable experience. It was his first trip abroad, and it was one of his first real opportunities to compare his own ability with that of the best players in the world. Someone once said: "No defeat that you learn something from is a real loss." Arthur proved that to be true.

At the National Clay Court Championships in Chicago, he snapped back to score a win over the highly ranked Chris Crawford.

It was not a simple victory, for it marked a great improvement in Arthur's play. Once a slam-bang player whose greatest weapon was his power serve, Arthur's game suddenly showed more imagination. No longer was he just serving the ball hard, then rushing to the net to score on a sharp volley. Instead, he was opening a bag full of tricks, using many different shots.

On a clay tennis court the ball bounces more slowly than it does on either a grass or a concrete surface. To do his best on it, a player needs to fix his mind firmly on the game and must not slam his shots back over the net. Until now, Arthur had been weak at this kind of play. But against Crawford, he kept his mind firmly on the game. He took his time and placed his drives carefully, moving his shots about the court fast enough to keep Crawford at a constant disadvantage.

The week after beating Crawford, Arthur moved on to the grass courts at the Merion Cricket Club, near Philadelphia. Here he had the pleasure of upsetting two players who had beaten him before—Marty Riessen and the National Intercollegiate Champion, Allen Fox. Arthur put them both out of the tournament, Riessen one day and Fox the next. But he then had to face the player who had beaten him at Wimbledon—Chuck McKinley.

With a strong service that skidded on the grass, Arthur jumped ahead, taking six of the first seven games to win the first set 6–1. People sat in shocked silence as they watched what appeared to have the making of a national upset.

As the second set began, Arthur lost some of his drive. The sharp edge left his game. "What's happening?" he asked himself. "You beat the Number 1 player in the country 6–1. Now get going. Beat him the second set."

But Arthur never did get going. McKinley went on to take the match and, later, the tournament.

Though he had lost to McKinley, the tennis world realized that Arthur Ashe was a name to watch. He was now ranked Number 18 in the United States. The only Negro in tennis history to have gained greater recognition was Althea Gibson. Tennis people wondered if Arthur might be chosen for the Davis Cup Team—the first Negro ever to be so honored.

So complete had been the change in Arthur Ashe himself that the talk about his making the Davis Cup Team no longer seemed to him to be foolish. The dream he and Ronald Charity had hardly dared to mention out loud now seemed a real possibility.

If he could keep up the pace of his play, the committee would have a difficult time not selecting him.

Then suddenly Arthur ran into trouble. With the first Davis Cup match against Mexico only weeks away, he entered the Eastern Grass Court Championships at Orange, New Jersey, and lost to Gene Scott.

Scott, too, was noted for his big serve, but Arthur had no trouble handling it until late in the match. He took the first set and lost the second. In the third, he had a comfortable lead of 4–1, when it happened. He began to find it more and more difficult to return Scott's service. From then on, it was down hill all the way. Nothing he tried seemed to do any good. On the final point, he hit Scott's serve into the net and the match was over. Gene Scott had won.

Upset both by the match and the thought that he had probably blown his chances of being selected for the Davis Cup, Arthur headed for the shower room. All that he had worked for so hard now seemed out of reach.

But as he sat in the stands later that afternoon watching some of the other matches, Harcour Woods, the chairman of the Davis Cup Committee, came over to Arthur.

"Art," Mr. Woods said, smiling, "I am happy to tell you for myself and for the committee that you have been selected to play with the Davis Cup Team. It won't be in the newspapers until tomorrow, but I thought I'd tell you today."

News of the "first Negro Davis Cupper" was too good to keep. It spread quickly to the sports reporters at the Orange Lawn Tennis Club that day, and stories soon followed in the newspapers.

Arthur Ashe was big news and, naturally, the reporters had questions to ask him. Gene Scott, who had beaten Arthur the day before in the Easterns, had not made the team, and a few people wondered if Arthur was chosen only because of his color.

"Do you think they picked you because you are a Negro?" one newspaper reporter asked.

Arthur, who seldom showed any temper in public, could not hide his anger. He thought back to the thousands of hours of practice he had put in and the hundreds of tennis matches he had played to reach this point in his career.

"Just check the won and lost records," he snapped at the reporter.

If being named to the Davis Cup Team was an honor, being a member of it was just more hard work, Arthur discovered. Never in his life had he been subjected to such rough training. It seemed as though the better he got, the harder he had to train.

"I don't go for all that six A.M. chopping wood and lifting weights and running through parks. I go crazy," Arthur confessed to a sports writer long afterward. "When the team captain asks me to go out and hit, sometimes I say, 'Aw, let's talk about it.'"

Since he was six feet tall and weighed only 150 pounds, he had little difficulty keeping in shape for normal play.

"It doesn't take much for me to get in condition," he once explained to a reporter. "In about a week's time, if I ran, skipped rope, ate, and went to bed early, I would be ready to play a five-set match. Some of the bigger players would probably have to work a lot harder."

Nevertheless, as a Davis Cupper Arthur found he had to work daily to condition himself. There was no sleeping late in the mornings. By eight A.M. the members of the team were up for a breakfast of bacon and eggs—no bread. In fact, no bread was served during the entire training period. The good qualities of bread could be found in other foods, it was explained, and bread took up too much space in the stomach.

Most players also had hot cereal and skimmed milk for their first meal of the day, although Arthur was allowed to drink whole milk because of his lean frame.

Besides all the hard work, the Davis Cup training periods provided Arthur with one of the greatest thrills of his life, for the team coach was none other than his hero, Pancho Gonzales.

"Gonzales won't even let me step on the court before I skip rope for fifteen minutes," Arthur exclaimed, when asked about the training program. "Then I have to run the distance of a football field three times. Then I can hit just certain shots, fifteen minutes each, for an hour and a half."

This was only the morning's activity. Such exercises were designed to strengthen and loosen the players' muscles.

At noon they paused for a light lunch of meat and fruit and a rest period during which they could watch TV, read, or take a nap. The deadly serious practice periods came in the afternoon when players were required to go all out in matches that might last for three or four sets.

Dinner was at six or seven in the evening, and team members were expected to be in bed no later than midnight.

In spite of all the preparation, Arthur found himself warming the bench during the first match against Mexico. He wasn't the least bit bothered, though. In a way, he was almost glad.

"My greatest fear is losing a Davis Cup match," he explained. "When I lose one, it will show in the record book that the United States lost. I don't want to be the cause of that. It's funny. This is what you shoot for so long, and when it comes, you are nervous."

Arthur was later to realize that there was no disgrace in losing, even in a Davis Cup match.

It wasn't until the U.S. team was playing Venezuela that Arthur finally got into action. The matches were held at Denver, Colorado, and Arthur was pitted against Orlando Bracamonte.

In each Davis Cup meeting five matches are played: four singles and one double. A team must win any three of the five contests to gain the victory. When Arthur took to the court to play Bracamonte, there was no pressure on him to win, except his own desire to prove himself. By that time the United States had already won enough matches to take the tournament.

Still, for Arthur it was his first Davis Cup competition, and he geared himself to do well. He beat Bracamonte in straight sets, losing only two games to him.

Arthur knew it now—he was a Davis Cup player at last.

Chapter 11

THE SHADOW OF DOUBT

Arthur entered the 1964 season as the sixth ranked amateur tennis player in the United States. He was riding high. On his college team at U.C.L.A. he held the Number 1 position, and he had been elected one of the captains by his team mates. In rankings on the Pacific Coast, he was second only to Dennis Ralston, hero of the University of Southern California's tennis team, and even Dennis Ralston had bowed to Arthur on more than one occasion.

In the Southern California Intercollegiate matches, Arthur defeated Ralston after three long, tough sets that lasted some two and a half hours. It was no sudden change in his game that brought Arthur the victory that day. He had fought every minute he was on the court, coming from behind to win, 5–7, 6–4, 8–6.

Then, in the Southern California Sectional Championship and the Big Six Intercollegiate

Tournament that followed, it was Ralston's turn. He beat Arthur both times.

In June, Arthur went back to England to the grass courts at Wimbledon. After a slow start, he managed to defeat the Czechoslovakian champion, Milan Holececk, Cliff Richey of Texas, and another American, Bill Bond.

Then, as had happened the year before, Arthur met defeat at the hands of the player who was to win the tournament. This time it was Roy Emerson of Australia. Roy was then, without question, the world's top amateur player, and he beat Arthur in straight sets.

It was a tremendous experience playing Emerson. He hit hard and had an excellent all around game. Fast as Arthur was, Emerson was faster. Arthur's serve would go booming into the court, but Emerson's returns would come booming right back, often winning the point. The only other American player who lasted longer in the tournament was the defending champion, Chuck McKinley. But if Arthur had to lose, at least he lost to the best. In fact, his play at Wimbledon impressed everyone.

After Arthur returned home he continued to improve. In the Pennsylvania Grass Court Championships, it took the rough, tough Chuck McKinley thirty-six games to beat the young Negro from

Richmond. The score was 10–8, 10–8, and McKinley had to pour it on to win.

It was a good warm-up for Arthur, who went on to play next in the Eastern Grass Court Championships at Orange, New Jersey. There he was one of six players who ranked in the top ten of American amateur tennis. In the quarter finals, Arthur met his old Pacific Coast rival, Dennis Ralston. The first set seemed to last forever before Denny took it, 15–13. But then Denny let up, and Arthur made good use of his cannon ball serve and long hard drives to the base line to take the next two sets and the match.

In the semi-finals, Arthur faced the defending champion, Gene Scott, who had beaten Arthur the year before, but had failed to be selected for the Davis Cup Team. Now, as though to make up for his earlier defeat by Scott, Arthur gave it everything he had, beating Scott in straight sets.

Only Clark Graebner now stood between Arthur and winning the tournament. But Graebner was quite a problem. His record was every bit as good as Arthur's. He could hit the ball well and with power. In their match, Arthur managed to take Graebner's serve three times in the four sets, while Graebner took Ashe's serve only once. The difference favored Arthur, and it proved just enough for him to win, 4–6, 8–6, 6–4, 6–3.

It was a surprising performance, and it earned

Arthur an invitation to play in the National Championships at Forest Hills.

There he won three matches before losing in the quarter finals to Australia's Tony Roche. He didn't become the champion, but, as it turned out, he was soon to win a real victory—that victory came right after the Nationals, while Arthur was in Cleveland, Ohio, with the U. S. Davis Cup Team.

The U.S. was playing its Challenge Round against Australia, and things did not go well. The American boys lost 3–2. Although Arthur did not get a chance to play in Cleveland, he had become known for his good court manners and his attitude toward the game. As someone once said, "Instead of throwing his racket when he misses a shot, he might get mad enough to mutter 'Boy, oh boy' to himself."

So right after the matches, Arthur was presented with the United States' highest tennis prize, the Johnston Award, given each year to the player who exhibits courtesy, character, and a spirit of cooperation. The winner must also be a good sport and be willing to help younger players contribute to the growth of tennis.

Arthur was thrilled. "I hope I can prove to be the exception to the rule that 'good guys' always finish last," he joked, covering up his feelings as the prize was presented to him. The people in the stands were delighted with Arthur.

And they had reason to be. Arthur's prize was quite an occasion in the records of American tennis. Tennis was looked on as a gentleman's sport, a game played by rich boys. The members of the private tennis clubs were as white as the T-shirts and shorts they wore. Any Negroes seen at the clubs in those days were either waiters or maids.

Now, in 1964, Arthur Ashe—a twenty-one-year-old "colored" boy from Richmond, Virginia (where Negroes were still not welcome in private tournaments)—stood in the center court at Cleveland to receive his prize as a gentleman.

Arthur often found it difficult to deal with the fact that dark skin was odd in a white world. He was a tennis player who happened to be a Negro, he insisted, not a Negro tennis player.

Nevertheless, his presence frequently caused more than a slight social ripple. Privately, some hosts of parties that were given after the matches wondered "what to do with Arthur Ashe." They soon found, however, that if he was treated like any other guest, Arthur would enjoy himself.

"I'm simply me and not something strange," he tried to explain.

But other Negroes did not always understand what Arthur's life was like.

As he described the situation: "I've found that tennis does affect my social life. During the spring, I don't see anybody but people in the world of tennis. Some of the Negroes around the college will talk about you if they think you don't want to associate with your own people."

No matter which way Arthur turned he seemed to be in an odd situation. "Even when I am with nice white people, they are usually bending over backwards to be too nice. They want to keep making sure that I'm feeling good, just because I'm a Negro. Then there are the Negroes who keep giving me advice: Don't trust the white man."

More important to Arthur than how he was accepted in society were certain things he wanted to do for the young people of his race. He hoped to do his part by showing others the way, as Jackie Robinson had done, and Willie Mays, Wilt Chamberlain, Bill Russell, and Jimmy Brown. Arthur realized that if he allowed any of the social problems he might run into to really "bug" him, he would never be able to do these things.

First of all, Arthur Ashe was a tennis player, and his greatest responsibility was to make himself as expert at the game as possible. When the 1965 amateur rankings were announced by the U.S.L.T.A., Arthur was named to the Number 3 spot—third best in the country. Only Dennis Ralston and Chuck McKinley were rated above him.

In a sense, tennis players who gain such positions are like the bad men of the Old West. Once they get their reputations, everybody wants to knock them off.

Arthur noted this when he said, "As soon as I got that Number 3 ranking, I became fair game for every tournament player in the country."

So he did, and in short order he was beaten in the Philadelphia Indoor Invitational, the National Indoor Championships, and the Western Intercollegiate Indoor Championships. In each case he lost before he reached the final round.

After watching one defeat, Arthur's old coach, Doctor Johnson, remarked, "Arthur's trouble now is that he has too many shots, and on the lightning fast indoor surface, he makes up his mind one sixty-fourth of a second too late which shot to use."

Arthur had another explanation. "My biggest problem is fixing my mind on the game," he said. "I slide through too many matches. I usually work just enough to win. That's bad. Tennis is built on split second timing and quick thinking. Thoughts come to me too often out there on the court, and I take my mind off the game.

"Some people are saying that I don't fight—that maybe I quit when the going gets rough. But I can fight all right."

Arthur could fight, and he proved it. He bounced back from his losses to win two California tournaments and the Big Six Athletic Association of Western Universities title.

No one could deny that Arthur was on the winning trail again, but many people felt that his play was not as brilliant as it once had been. They began to wonder if Arthur would ever become a truly great player or if he was just another kid who had almost made it big.

Chapter 12

VICTORY AT DALLAS

"Art, it looks as though it's all going to be up to you."

George MacCall, the captain of the United States Davis Cup Team, was talking. It was time for the first inter-zone challenge matches. There are three such zones—American, European, and Asian. A team must win the championship of its zone before it can challenge the winners of other titles and the nation that holds the cup, the nation that won it the previous year.

In the American Zone the United States was to play Canada, and the U.S. team had lost two of its strongest players.

Chuck McKinley had decided he couldn't spare the time to train for the Davis Cup matches. He felt he had to stick to his business career.

Dennis Ralston had been in a hot argument with the Davis Cup officials and had been "benched"— left off the team.

Captain MacCall had to go with Gene Scott and Arthur Ashe. Arthur, ranked Number 3 behind McKinley and Ralston, was now America's best hope.

Once more, Arthur prepared himself for the demands of the moment. As he stood for the ceremonies before the game on opening day at Bakersfield, California, he thought again of how much he would hate to lose at his country's expense.

In the first match against Canada's Keith Carpenter, Arthur blazed away. He smashed eleven service aces (a serve so fast and so well placed that the other player can't get his racket on it), winning 6–3, 6–3, 6–1, in an hour and ten minutes.

On the third day, with a United States victory already assured by his team mates' play, Ashe beat Canada's Harry Fauquier by the same score he had run up against Carpenter. If anything, Arthur played even better in his second match. Fauquier was never really in the game.

With a total of three Davis Cup victories now under his belt, Arthur returned to U.C.L.A. to take the National Intercollegiate Singles title and to team with Ian Crookenden to win the doubles.

Then, Wimbledon again. Arthur was used to playing on courts with hard surfaces. Moving from the hard courts to grass was always difficult. Still, he did well at Wimbledon, winning his first three matches before meeting Mexico's Rafael Osuna.

Back in 1963, when Arthur had first played Osuna, he had beaten him in two of three meetings, but this time the young Mexican took Ashe in three straight sets, 8–6, 6–4, 6–4.

After Wimbledon, Arthur began to slip, losing out in the first three tournaments he entered on his return to America. "Could he win again?" was the question most sports writers were asking as the Davis Cup matches with Mexico neared. With Osuna and Antonio Palafox to play the singles and doubles, Mexico had a strong team. The result was judged as a toss-up at best.

Ralston, back on the team, would do well, and he and Ham Richardson would make a strong doubles team. But Richardson wasn't getting any younger. For the last few years, his tennis had been limited to week ends and small tournaments in the southwestern area where he lived. No one was even sure whether Arthur would be called on to play against the Mexicans. Many felt he was a bad risk.

But Arthur's hero and coach, Pancho Gonzales, didn't agree at all.

"Arthur Ashe," Gonzales said, "is capable of beating anyone in the world."

Gonzales proved that he meant what he said. When the moment came, he suggested that team captain George MacCall name Arthur to one of the singles spots, along with Dennis Ralston. Few people felt that Gonzales had chosen wisely.

The draw for the opening match took place on August 2nd, the day the matches were to begin. Its result delighted the Mexicans. Twenty-one-year-old Arthur, least experienced of America's Davis Cuppers, was pitted against the twenty-six-year-old Osuna, most experienced of Mexico's team, the 1963 United States Champion, and a deadly player in Davis Cup competition.

"It's exactly what we wanted," beamed Pancho Contreras, captain of the Mexico team. "Winning the first match is a real advantage. Our idea is to get the first one of the five points."

Had Contreras known what had happened the night before the Ashe-Osuna match, he might have been even happier.

Arthur had gone to bed in his hotel before midnight, but a loud crowd having a late party kept him from any kind of sound sleep. Finally, at five o'clock in the morning, Arthur decided to get up. It made no sense to try to sleep when all he could think of was the match ahead of him that day.

When George MacCall came in to Arthur's room at 8:15, he asked him how he had slept. Arthur told him that it had been one of the most peaceful nights he had spent in a long time. (As

Arthur explained later, "We try not to get George too excited.")

Though Arthur had had little sleep, he did have three things going for him that day: spirit, conditioning, and cool nerve. He had to be called away from a game of tic-tac-toe with his team mate Frank Froehling before the draw, matching him against Osuna that August 2nd afternoon in Dallas, Texas.

Arthur had one other thing going for him, too. Osuna had been operated on the winter before for a bad knee, and he was having some difficulty covering the court quickly.

When the official announced that Ashe would be playing against him, Osuna laughed and threw his arms around Arthur.

"Well, the two little brown bodies will meet first," he said.

Onto the cement court at the new Samuell-Grand Tennis Center the two young men walked. Cement surfaces are slower than grass, and Arthur knew that his game was at its best on the faster grass surface. He would have to be careful here.

No doubt those people who had seen Arthur Ashe play before were as surprised as Osuna was by the style he now showed. Instead of hitting for winners, Arthur placed his shots carefully and his timing was perfect.

Again and again Osuna was caught out of position as Ashe hit a fine passing shot or a backhand drive to the far corner, leaving Osuna flat-footed.

Arthur's serve was working extremely well—both his cannon ball and his spinning serves. During the match, he served fifteen aces. Time after time, he hit low volleys for winners.

Osuna, a very good and clever player, was rarely up to Arthur's game. Even when his first serve was working, it didn't have the power of Arthur's. Usually fast on his feet and seldom if ever bothered by the thought of losing, Osuna's confidence quickly left him. Even in the last set, when he came back strongly, he was not playing as well as he generally did. The operation on his knee had slowed him down.

All Arthur's hard training was finally paying off. He was sure that he would not tire, and he pushed himself to keep Osuna out of position. In an hour and thirty-five minutes it was over. Arthur had beaten Osuna, 6–2, 6–3, 9–7.

George MacCall was delighted. "Today Arthur became a man," he exclaimed. "He was under great pressure, and he came through."

Arthur, who was usually last to speak and neither muttered in defeat nor crowed in victory, could not hide his pleasure this time.

"I feel wonderful," he confessed.

Winning the first match in the series of five was

a big advantage, and that advantage—thanks to Arthur Ashe—now belonged to the Americans.

As expected, Denny Ralston won his singles match, too, downing Antonio Palafox, Mexico's second finest player. But the U.S. doubles team of Ralston and Richardson had tougher sledding. The Mexicans were not out of it yet. Osuna and Palafox beat the American doubles team in a long and hard fought match.

The score in the team matches now stood at 2–1, with the Americans ahead and two more singles matches still to be played. This time Ashe would meet Palafox and Ralston would play Osuna. Again the pressure was on Arthur to win for his country.

It was a hot day in Dallas, and it seemed even hotter on the cement surface of the court as Ashe and Palafox began to warm up for their match. The crowd cheered them both as they moved around on the court. Everyone seemed certain that this match was going to be a good one.

And it was—at least for the first three games of the first set. Both players hit the ball fiercely, with streaking services and sharp forehands and back-hands down the line and cross court. In both the first and third games, Palafox put Arthur to the test, just missing two opportunities to break service. Then, suddenly, Palafox seemed to fade away.

Arthur was playing with even more power than

he had against Osuna, and his control was perfect. In one game in the second set he served four straight aces against the Mexican. The final score, 6–1, 6–4, 6–4, did not completely reflect Arthur's play. As it became clear to him that Palafox had lost his spirit, Arthur began to take all kinds of chances, hitting wildly for points. Often he tried to drive Palafox's serves back for winners, and too frequently he over hit or under hit, driving the ball either out of the court or into the net.

"It was his booming serve," Palafox said sadly, when it was all over. "I tried to upset his timing, but I couldn't."

So Arthur, who hadn't been counted on for much help, actually led the United States team to victory. Mexico's team captain Pancho Contreras put it well when he said, "There was no way to defeat Ashe. We didn't expect him to be so strong. He was the weak side that turned out to be the strong side."

From Dallas, the U.S. team went on to challenge Spain on the clay courts at Barcelona. MacCall and Gonzales knew that Arthur's game was better suited to a fast surface like grass or cement, and they also knew that Manuel Santana, Spain's Number 1 player and the Number 1 amateur player in the world, was expert on clay. After much thought, they decided they would not play Arthur against the Spaniards. But Spain's team proved too much for the Americans, anyway. Santana and his team mate, Luis Arilla, easily beat Frank Froehling, Denny Ralston, and Clark Graebner.

After it was all over, the American Ambassador to Spain, Angier Biddle Duke, had the U.S. boys over for a party at his home.

"How would Ashe have done in the singles?" he asked.

"We are still wondering," came the reply.

But Arthur, who would have liked to play, and wondered frequently during the matches how he would have done, never felt the least slighted at being benched. He had already found his glory—in the summer sun at Dallas.

Chapter 13

ON HIS OWN

The victory at Dallas had proved one thing. It had proved that Arthur could play his best tennis under pressure.

Armed with new confidence, Arthur made his seventh trip to the grass courts of the West Side Tennis Club in Forest Hills to play in the Nationals. September in New York is often hotter than the other summer months, and so it was in 1965.

The world's best amateur tennis players had gathered at Forest Hills for the famous tournament: Roy Emerson and Fred Stolle of Australia, Manuel Santana of Spain, Rafael Osuna and Antonio Palafox of Mexico, Cliff Drysdale of South Africa, Dennis Ralston, Chuck McKinley, and Gene Scott of the United States.

Arthur had to play his old rival, Gene Scott, in the first round.

Arthur was at the top of his game. He beat Scott, then went on to defeat Gary Rose of California, King Lambert of New York, and Thomas Koch of Brazil. Of the four, Koch gave Arthur the hardest time, forcing him into a long, tiring battle. The final scores were 12–10, 13–11, 10–8.

When Arthur reached the quarter finals, the defending champion, Roy Emerson, awaited him. Like Ashe, Emerson was in rare form that September and had not lost a set in the tournament. Both players were full of confidence, Ashe because of his Davis Cup victories over Osuna and Palafox, and Emerson because he had just had the thrill of winning at Wimbledon.

Some eleven thousand fans jammed the stadium at Forest Hills to watch the young American Negro take on the twenty-eight-year-old Australian. The crowd that filled the stands that day expected Arthur Ashe to do little more than give the famous Emerson a good run for his money.

Before the match, Arthur got some valuable advice on how to play Emerson from a past United States Indoor and Wimbledon champion, Dick Savitt.

"Crack those returns of service," Savitt told him. "Everyone just chips them back against Emerson. Don't do it. Hit them, hit them, hit them!"

When the time came to appear on court, Arthur

told everyone who questioned him that he was ready and had confidence.

Above the steps that lead from the porch to the courts at Forest Hills are two lines from Rudyard Kipling's poem, *If*. The sign on which these words appear faces the inside of the porch, so that each player may read them before he steps onto the court:

> *If I can meet with triumph and disaster,*
> *And treat those two imposters just the same.*

As Arthur passed under the sign, keyed up for his coming match, he read the words again. They reminded him of the things his father used to tell him, that it was the way you played that was important, not who won. Part of doing a thing well was learning that sometimes you had to lose, and that you could learn from your losses how to improve. Arthur walked onto the court to the crowd's wild cheers.

In the first set, both Emerson and Ashe fought as hard as they could. It lasted seventy minutes and twenty-four games, before Arthur won, 13–11. Forest Hills hadn't known such excitement in years.

Arthur had had trouble with his first serve—the cannon ball—at the beginning, so he switched from the flat serve to a spin and let up a little. The new serve worked just right. And as Savitt had advised, he blasted every return of Emerson's service he could get his racket on, hitting flat forehands and over spin backhands to keep Emerson constantly on the run.

Arthur was playing brilliantly and with imagination. He was forcing Emerson to go to the net whether or not it was the right place to be. Only Emerson's excellent volley shots kept him in the match.

As the match continued, Arthur talked to himself. "Come on, come on, keep your eye on the ball, keep your eye on the ball. Hit your forehand, hit your forehand. Up for the overhead, up for the overhead."

Arthur was thundering through Emerson and he was doing so by using his ground strokes as his chief weapon.

Only once in the match did Arthur let up. That was in the third set, when Emerson came back to win it. But the loss of one set didn't matter. After two hours and forty-five minutes of great tennis, Arthur had upset the man considered one of the finest amateur players in the world, 13–11, 6–4, 10–12, 6–2.

The sports writers were delighted by Arthur's victory, perhaps more so than the young hero himself. "We are tired of interviewing Australian winners," one reporter said.

However, Arthur was no real winner yet. "One match doesn't prove a thing," he replied. "You have to establish a pattern of winning. That's what Emerson has been doing for years."

Arthur seemed to be right. The following day he was beaten in the next to last round by Spain's great Manuel Santana.

This time it was Santana who was not expected to do well in the competition. Santana was Spain's best player, but he was used to playing on clay, not on grass. Many people thought that he would be too slow on the faster surface and fail to return skidding, cannon ball serves.

Another huge crowd came to the stadium for the match between Ashe and Santana, and the fans greeted Arthur's appearance warmly. As he had done on the previous day, Arthur won the first set with a powerful attack. Sharp backhands and forehands whistled up the lines for winners. His first service was smashing in, and he was hitting strong backhand and forehand volleys that Santana could not reach. The stands roared with delight. Arthur seemed on his way to another victory.

The second set was a very different matter. Santana was a changed player, and he took command of the match from that point on. Here, on the grass of Forest Hills, he displayed the great skills he had always shown on clay courts. Time after time he hit shots that were just out of Arthur's reach and forced Arthur into errors on low volleys at the net.

Even Santana's serve increased in pace. The starch had gone out of Arthur's game.

It took Santana nearly two hours, but he finally won in four sets, 2–6, 6–4, 6–2, 6–4. Playing against such a master was a bitter but valuable tennis education for Arthur Ashe.

Later in the year Arthur beat another famous Australian, Fred Stolle, ranked Number 2 among the world's amateur tennis players. Their meeting occurred in the finals of the Colonia National Invitation Tournament at Fort Worth, Texas. Then, as if to prove that his victories over Emerson and Stolle had not been luck, Arthur teamed with Ham Richardson to whip the two Australians in the doubles, 3–6, 14–12, 6–4.

As winter neared, Arthur returned to California and school. He had long since decided to list his name at tournaments as Arthur Ashe of Los Angeles rather than Arthur Ashe of Richmond. He couldn't feel that his tennis home was Richmond, where he had been denied the right to play on the courts at Grant Park. He reminded himself that even now he was not welcome in matches in Virginia, if indeed he would even be permitted to enter them. He didn't really feel any hate because of it. He just wanted to forget the past and begin again in a place where he knew he was accepted.

At fifteen, he had been the Number 5 junior player in the country. Now, at twenty-two, he was Number 3 in the United States and Number 6 in the world. And from here on in he was on his own. How much success or failure he experienced would be up to him. Knowing his own strengths and weaknesses was more important than ever now, and he faced them frankly in an interview with a magazine writer.

"I've always been soft, actually, afraid to speak up at times," Arthur admitted. "I try to please everybody, and it can't be done. But I am very easy going, and it takes a lot to make me mad.

"People take advantage of me because of this, and sometimes, deep down inside, I wish I were somewhere else, but I don't say anything.

"I think that's the reason I play tennis the way I do. I know that no matter how I look at myself, my personality is that of a calm, easy going guy who really doesn't care too much about anything on the surface. But deep down inside I hate to be given instructions about how to do things. So when I play tennis, I play it my own way.

"I am still talked about for hitting too many crazy shots. These shots frequently pull me out of trouble spots, but more often they get me into deeper trouble. Yet I continue to do it.

"Perhaps the only reason for doing it is that I have come this far, why change now? I know this is not the proper way to look at it, but my very style of play is my way of coming out with it: *If you don't like it, that's too bad,* I am saying. I am out there on my own."

His mental attitude was not the only thing Arthur tried to make clear for the writer that day. There was also the matter of actual tennis play.

"Before I had the serve, I had the backhand," Arthur explained. "All of my strokes stem from the days when I was so small that I couldn't swing the racket properly. I used to sling it through the air, depending on the racket to do all the work.

"Other players can hit their forehand twice as hard as I can, but they never hit a backhand as hard as I do. This is mainly because when you hit a forehand, you swing the racket toward your body. With your backhand, you swing the racket away from your body. In the forehand, any force you get behind the ball has to be mostly from your arm and shoulder. But with the backhand, you can get a big back swing and whip the racket around.

"I sling the racket almost like I was swatting a fly. Of course, if you can develop timing with this, it makes a great shot."

Tennis was no longer just a game to him, Arthur admitted. Now it was a whole way of life.

"Everybody wants recognition," he said. "You like seeing your name in the papers, you like hearing it on TV and radio. Tennis is the only way I can do it. I can't do it making speeches, or playing baseball, or acting in the movies.

"It is also a means to an end. If you are pretty well known, chances are somebody will want you and pay for your services later on—pay much more than if you are a nobody."

At the end of 1965 Arthur believed that he had reached another level in his career: "You always have doubts because you never progress in a straight line," he explained. "It is like steps, actually. You go up, and then you reach a plateau and then you go up again, and reach another plateau, and so on.

"But the higher you go, the longer the plateaus get, because the competition is stiffer up there. One good thing is, as you go higher, there are fewer and fewer people who are your equals at that stage. Then, the competition is so tough and the type of play so high, it takes a lot more skill to reach a higher plateau.

"Occasionally you break through here and there, and you gain confidence. You develop new shots, and other shots that were difficult for you before begin to come a little easier. You feel better on the court. Your mental attitude toward the game changes. You realize that you can beat some

117

players just playing at half speed because they are afraid of you. You are a bigger name, so they walk on the court figuring that they are going to lose. And they do lose."

But Arthur had no doubts about what he had not accomplished. "I haven't done anything really *big* yet," he said. "I knocked out a top player in a big match, but I didn't win the tournament. Next year, somebody will be expecting me to win one of the Big Four titles—the French, Australian, English, or American.

"I have reached the stage where I can win one of those tournaments, but until I do, I will still be on this plateau where I am now. I haven't put my game together strongly enough to come through with the really big win."

The time was coming when Arthur would have a shot at a series of really big wins. He would get his first chance in a tour of Australia. There it would all be up to him.

Chapter 14

HOME TO RICHMOND

When Arthur Ashe went off to Australia, American tennis fans awaited word of how he was doing in the land where tennis is the national sport.

The news was big.

Arthur won the Queensland Championships in Brisbane, and slammed his way to the finals of the New South Wales tournament before bowing out. He was off to a good start, and there were still five more tournaments to go.

In his third, the Victorian in Melbourne, Arthur was stopped short of the finals by an American team mate, Herb FitzGibbon. But he marched to victory in his next three tournaments. First, in Adelaide, then in the Western Australian Championships, and finally in the Tasmanian Championships in Hobart.

Twice during the tour, Arthur met and defeated the world's top-ranked amateur, Australian Roy Emerson. But in the Australian Nationals at Sydney, when the two once again were face to face in the finals, Emerson proved he deserved his ranking and fought through to win.

It was an important match for Arthur, and he began his play as though he would sweep Emerson off the court. But he could not keep up the pace. Balls went long and into the net, and down the line shots fell wide of their mark. He was aced by Emerson; he missed easy shots. It was just one of those days.

Still, of the seven tournaments, Arthur had taken four and reached the finals in all but one.

As Arthur toured Australia, sports writers at home began to think about his future. He would soon be graduated from U.C.L.A., and he seemed a natural for the small group of professional tennis players who tour the world. Not only was Arthur an unusually fine tennis player, he was a sure drawing card.

One thing they forgot, however, was that Arthur was also a member of a unit of the Reserve Officers Training Corps, and his country was currently engaged in a war in Vietnam.

"The Army has first call on me when I graduate," Arthur announced in Australia. "I will be proud to serve in Vietnam. If there is a job to be done out there, the sooner it is over, the better."

Arthur made his way back home—not just to

the United States, but to Richmond, where there was a surprising tribute waiting for him on February 4, 1966—"Arthur Ashe Day." Richmond, the city which had paid no attention to the rising young tennis star, was now ready to honor its native son as the most famous international athlete in its history.

On the plane ride home, Arthur thought of all the times he had wanted to play against white boys in Richmond and had been refused. He remembered places he had wanted to go and things he had wanted to see in Richmond which were not open to him because of his color. Now he was flying home to take part in a day the city officials had set aside in his honor.

It was late evening when Arthur's plane touched down in Virginia. From the field he was taken to the city's most famous hotel, the John Marshall, where bellboys addressed him as "Sir." The bed he slept in that night could never have been his when he had lived in Richmond only six short years ago.

The morning after he arrived, Arthur went before the State Legislature, where he was introduced by Delegate J. Sargeant Reynolds and where a resolution was offered for the General Assembly to express its good wishes to Arthur for his continued success.

In the afternoon, he was taken to the Richmond

City Hall. There Mayor Morrill Crowe presented him with a copy of the City Council's resolution, passed a month earlier, proclaiming the date as "Arthur Ashe Day."

Some two hundred citizens were present as the mayor declared:

"This city is known around the world for many products—cigarettes . . . statesmen . . . and now Arthur Ashe, who has carried his country's banner around the world with dignity, honor, and skill."

While the mayor could speak only of what he had learned from written accounts, there was a man present in Richmond on that day who could give expert information on Arthur Ashe, and his conduct on and off the courts. At the dinner for Arthur that evening, Davis Cup team captain George MacCall did speak out:

"Arthur is one of the finest ambassadors this country has ever had," MacCall said, and then went on to give his impression of the well mannered boy with whom he had been working for two years.

Earlier, MacCall had brought the sports writers up to date on Arthur's tennis play. "It is hard to compare players," said MacCall. "But everything has improved with Arthur—his game and his confidence. Everything has changed. He has more experience. I think that Arthur, more than any other player I have known, is sure of his ability.

122

"Last summer Rafael Osuna beat him in straight sets at Wimbledon. Arthur had had trouble getting to London. It was tough getting a plane to New York from the West Coast, where he had first won the National Intercollegiate Championship. Arthur didn't arrive in London until ten o'clock the night before his first round match, and he lost.

"Still, three weeks after losing to Osuna, Arthur played him again in the Cup matches in Dallas and beat him. From that point on, Arthur has improved greatly.

"His tour in Australia was very successful. His play was something to watch."

MacCall was not the only one to sing Arthur's praises. There were his two earliest coaches, Ronald Charity and Doctor R. Walter Johnson, and his tennis buddies, Charles Pasarell, Frank Froehling, Chuck McKinley, Ian Crookenden, and Cliff Richey.

Another Richmond tennis player, Bitsy Harrison, who would never have been able to play against Arthur on the home courts in the old days, said of his rival: "When you play Arthur, you know that if you don't play your very best you will be beaten by him—but in the most gracious manner possible."

As the group gathered to honor Arthur at dinner that evening, the slender young man—now ranked as Number 2 in the United States—

expressed his thanks, showing the sense of humor that had carried him through some of the toughest moments of his life.

"Richmond has changed quite a bit," he said. Then he paused, and went on, "Your winters are worse."

But he was serious when he added: "Ten years ago this would not have happened. It is as much of a tribute to Richmond and the State of Virginia as it is to me."

Arthur Ashe had left Richmond a fair tennis player and had returned a hero. Soon, he realized, he would be leaving home again, this time for the Army.

For two years Arthur would have to concentrate on Army duties, without much time to play tennis. It seemed that Arthur might never reach his goals in tennis.

Then came 1968, the most incredible year in tennis history.

Chapter 15

TENNIS CHAMPION

Lieutenant Arthur Ashe stood ready to serve on the forecourt at Wimbledon, London's famous tennis club, in the world's most glamorous tennis tournament. It was July 1, 1968. The day was overcast; a cool mist filled the air. Across the net waited John Newcombe, defending Wimbledon champion, easy winner of the U.S. Nationals the previous year at Forest Hills, fourth seeded now—and a professional!

As Arthur prepared to toss up the ball he wondered for a split second whether it was fair to be pitted against a pro. Nobody else in all past Wimbledon tournaments had had to do this. But the thought disappeared as quickly as it had come. Only months before, world tennis had voted to allow "open" tennis. Professionals would play against amateurs in most of the world's big tournaments. Arthur realized that this was the shot in the arm that tennis badly needed. Besides, if he were ever going to win at Wimbledon, it would be meaningful only if the world's best players were entered.

Arthur tossed the ball high over his head, rose up after it, twisted his back, and let fly. The ball barreled forward, struck the tape of the net, and fell to the side. "Fault!" boomed the voice of the referee. The crowd murmured. Although Arthur had taken the first set from Newcombe 6–4, he was in trouble. Big John had service break point now, and was crouching low, preparing to drive Arthur's softer second serve for a winner.

Arthur couldn't let Newcombe get the advantage at this point. "Here goes," he said quietly. The ball went up, the racket whipped forward—as fast as ever. Newcombe was trapped. The ball screamed past his outstretched racket for an ace.

It was the shot Arthur needed. He went on to win the set 6–4. He lost the next two 4–6, 1–6, but in the final set he once again took command. Time and again Arthur was close to breaking Newcombe, but time and again Newcombe fought back. Then Arthur finally did break through with a backhand down the line. Holding service, he won the match with an ace, his thirteenth of the contest. Arthur had advanced to the quarter-finals at Wimbledon.

The next day Arthur faced Tom Okker, the "Flying Dutchman" from The Netherlands. Arthur's serve once again was the deciding factor and the Dutch player bowed 7–9, 9–7, 9–7, 6–2. Along with Arthur in the semi-finals was team mate Clark Graebner. It was a high moment for American tennis.

Arthur's semi-finalist opponent was Rod Laver, the world's best tennis player. Suddenly it was all over. Arthur played well but lost to a better player. Laver was still the world champion, but Arthur Ashe, by losing, made his point. As an amateur and part-time tennis player, he had made the semi-finals in an open tournament.

Now, the Army giving him more time, he would be able to concentrate on his game. Ahead was the United States Amateur Championships, a lifetime goal for Arthur.

"This is rough." Arthur sat down wearily in the dressing room at the Longwood Cricket Club in Brookline, Massachusetts, where the U.S. Amateurs were taking place.

"Yeah, I know what you mean," Ron Holmberg answered. Ron was Arthur's partner in the doubles and the pair had just been defeated. "But you'll do all right in the singles."

"Sure am tired, though."

It had only been a week since Arthur and the rest of the Davis Cup team of Clark Graebner, Stan Smith, and Bob Lutz had returned triumphantly from beating Spain in the Interzone semi-finals. Now Arthur was playing in both the singles and the doubles in the amateur championships. He tried to keep his mind off next week and the start of the U.S. Open, the richest, largest, and most important American tournament.

Ron was talking to him again. "You won easily enough today in the singles. What were the scores against Allan Stone?"

"3–6, 7–5, 9–7, 6–3. That wasn't so easy."

"Yes, but you're on a hot streak. I don't think there is anybody who will stop you."

That was another thing Arthur tried not to think about—the hot streak. Since a loss in the National Clay Court Championships, Arthur had not been beaten in close to twenty matches.

The following day, a hot August 24, Arthur kept his string alive by beating Jim McManus in four exciting sets, 6–4, 6–3, 14–16, 6–3. Once again service was his key to victory. Arthur would now go against Bob Lutz, Davis Cup teammate, who had already beaten Cliff Richey, Bob Hewitt, and powerful Clark Graebner. A victory tomorrow would wipe away three years of being Number 2. Arthur would be at the top of the nation's amateurs—Number 1 at last.

"Fool," Arthur told himself fiercely, tossing his racket down near the referee's stand and reaching for a towel. Bob Lutz headed for the alleyway that would take him to the locker room, a shower, and a change of clothes. In ten minutes the fourth set of the U.S. Amateurs finals would begin, Lutz leading two sets to one.

Arthur stayed where he was, toweling himself dry of the sweat that ninety-degree weather and three long sets of losing tennis had produced. He quickly changed shirts and waited angrily for Lutz to reappear.

"Don't you want to wash up and rest?" the referee asked.

"Nope. I just want to get going."

It was a highly unusual move, but Arthur was anxious to get back to the match. He did not want to relax mentally. He was determined not to let the top ranking slip away from him now. Not after all this time.

Bob Lutz came back from the locker room, ready to continue. After only a few shots into the fourth set, it became obvious to those watching that something about the match was different. Suddenly, it was all Ashe. Ace after ace tore off Arthur's racket. Winning volley after winning volley crashed past Lutz. Two sets later, the crown was Arthur's, 4–6, 6–3, 8–10, 6–0, 6–4. Richmond's most famous athlete had become the world's amateur tennis champion.

"Interesting, very interesting," Clark Graebner commented to Arthur as the two looked over the draw sheet at Forest Hills. The first United States Open was half over and both players had advanced successfully to the round of sixteen.

Graebner shook his head. "It's a rough field."

"Let's see," Arthur said, running his eyes down the long list of pairings, "tomorrow Newk plays Ulrich, Drysdale plays Laver, I play Emmo—I owe Mr. Emerson one—Rosewall meets Holmberg, Pancho—great, huh?—plays Roche, the Dutchman plays Curtis, Denny Ralston against Nikki Pilic, and you get Scott."

"Gene always does well in this tournament," Clark said.

"Sure, but look at me. Even if I beat Roy, Rod should beat Drysdale, and then it's me against Laver. You know what happened the last time?"

"Well, he's got that wrist problem," Clark offered.

"Thanks a lot."

The next day, September 5, Arthur Ashe played one of his finest games of tennis in beating Roy Emerson in straight sets, 6–4, 9–7, 6–3. Yet the match received only minor notice. Unbelievably, Cliff Drysdale defeated Rod Laver who was, it turned out, indeed bothered by a sprained wrist. Still, Drysdale was magnificent and would be almost as tough as the Australian would have been.

Arthur was eager for the match. There was more

to it than just playing in the quarter-finals. Cliff Drysdale came from South Africa, a country that openly practiced the belief that Negroes were inferior to whites. In South Africa, Negroes lived in the worst conditions imaginable. Wherever black men went they were required to carry passes or be thrown in jail.

Should Arthur play against Drysdale at all? Would it seem as if he were accepting the policies of that country? Arthur decided not. If he had refused to play, whatever protest he could make would be lost in the excitement of the tournament itself.

Arthur decided instead to meet the South African face-to-face—and beat him.

On September 5, Arthur Ashe conquered Cliff Drysdale, 8–10, 6–3, 9–7, 6–4.

Arthur and Clark Graebner clashed in the semi-finals in a match neither really wanted to play. It would mean a bitter defeat for one of America's Davis Cuppers. Graebner won the first set 6–4, and then the tension caught up with him. His game lost its fine edge and Arthur swept into the finals by taking the next three sets. Suddenly he found himself on the brink of a world championship. The two hottest players in the world would now meet for the right to be called the best, and one of them would be bent on revenge. Tomorrow Arthur would again meet the fabulous Flying Dutchman, Tom Okker.

"Come on, Ashe," Arthur muttered to himself, "let's get on top of things." Arthur bent low, leaned left, then right, as he waited for Okker's serve. It was the second game of the fifth and final set. Getting on top of things was something neither player had been able to do.

During a long first set in which the opponents had tried vainly to feel each other out, a service break and an ace had produced victory for Arthur. Okker's speed of foot and wrist gave him the second set 7–5. Then the players traded 6–3 sets. The first game of set five went to Arthur. The second game stood at 30-all as Okker rifled a serve toward Arthur and rushed the net.

Arthur's return came over low, forcing a shallow volley by Okker that Arthur lobbed over the Dutchman's head. Coming down, the ball raised chalk on the base line, just out of reach of the struggling Okker. At 30–40, a booming forehand passed Okker and Arthur had the all-important service break for a 2–0 lead. If he held serve the rest of the way, the match would be his.

At 4–2, service Ashe, the magic seemed to go out of Arthur's racket. At 30-all, Okker ran around a weak shot by Arthur, took it on his forehand, and drove it by the amateur champ. A single point now stood between Okker and a break, momentum enough to carry him to victory.

Arthur served, took the return on his forehand, and drove it wide and deep to Okker's backhand. Okker's return was out. Deuce.

Arthur's first serve missed, but he charged the net on his second and forced another backhand from Okker that failed again. And still again Arthur forced a backhand miss. The game was his.

Okker held service but was helpless against Arthur in the next game. A passing volley, an ace, and a forced backhand brought Arthur to 40–0 and match point. He stood for a brief moment, then served quickly. A strong volley, too fast for Okker, and the match was over. Arthur spun around, faced the wall, and crouched like a hungry tiger. Okker ran to the net where Arthur turned from his triumphant gesture and the two shook hands.

"Against you, my friend," Okker said smiling and shaking his head, "one doesn't get enough tennis. Congratulations."

Overcome for a minute, Arthur walked in circles behind the referee's stand, hands clasped high above his head. Moments later, he placed his hands on the back of his head, still walking around, and stared at the ground.

Asked by reporters after the match how he felt, Arthur replied, "It's nice to hear the announcer say, 'Point . . . Ashe,' but I'd rather hear him say, 'Point . . . United States.' "

Arthur had one more goal to achieve. More than anything, he wanted to return the Davis Cup to his country.

Early in November the Davis Cup team met India in the Interzone finals at Puerto Rico. On November 11, Arthur trounced Ramanathan Krishnan, India's best, 6–1, 6–3, 6–2 to clinch the series for America.

Then, during the Christmas holidays in Australia, Arthur swept to an easy victory over Ray Ruffles, smashing Australian morale and leading the squad to a 4–1 triumph—and ownership once again of the Davis Cup.

On the trip home Arthur tried to gather his thoughts. On February 24, he would be discharged from the Army. Already he had received fabulous offers to turn professional. In a short while, he might be earning as much as $100,000 a year.

He thought about the long, tough haul it had been to crack the white world of tennis, where the only Negroes to be found were waiters in the country clubs, where the best player in the land was often asked, "Boy, where's the men's room?", and where even the required dress was pure white. He thought about the fact that Negro kids might now begin to take up tennis seriously, would begin to fight their way onto any court they chose. He thought about the organizations he could join to lend his help and his name to the civil rights movement.

Then he leaned back in his comfortable jet seat and smiled. Nobody could stop him now. The world was his. His dreams had come true.

ARCHWAY
PAPERBACKS

Other titles you will enjoy

29707 JACKIE ROBINSON OF THE BROOKLYN DODGERS, by Milton J. Shapiro. Illustrated with photographs. The courageous black man who broke the color line in professional baseball and became one of the all-time greats of the Brooklyn Dodgers. (95¢)

29723 THE JIM THORPE STORY: *America's Greatest Athlete,* by Gene Schoor. Illustrated with photographs. The greatest all-around athlete of this century and his spectacular record in football, baseball, field and track. (95¢)

29606 THE STORY OF TY COBB: *Baseball's Greatest Player,* by Gene Schoor. Illustrated with photographs. The sports hero who overruled parental objection to play baseball, the thing he loved best, making history with his flaming spirit and amazing skill. (75¢)

29331 THE STRANGE INTRUDER, by Arthur Catherall. A reign of terror grips a remote, storm lashed island when a dangerous invader comes ashore. (60¢)

(If your bookseller does not have the titles you want, you may order them by sending the retail price, plus 25¢ (50¢ if you order two or more books) for postage and handling to: Mail Service Department, POCKET BOOKS, a division of Simon & Schuster, Inc., 1 West 39th Street, New York, N. Y. 10018. Please enclose check or money order—do not send cash.)

2975